R Graph Essentials

Use R's powerful graphing capabilities to design and create professional-level graphics

David Alexander Lillis

[PACKT] open source*

PUBLISHING community experience distilled

BIRMINGHAM - MUMBAI

R Graph Essentials

First published: September 2014

Production reference: 1150914

Published by Packt Publishing Ltd.
Livery Place
35 Livery Street
Birmingham B3 2PB, UK.

ISBN 978-1-78355-455-3

www.packtpub.com

Cover image by Arvind Shetty (arvindshetty86@gmail.com)

Credits

Author
David Alexander Lillis

Project Coordinator
Kartik Vedam

Reviewers
Mzabalazo Z. Ngwenya
Donato Teutonico
Tengfei Yin

Proofreaders
Simran Bhogal
Maria Gould
Ameesha Green

Commissioning Editor
Pramila Balan

Indexer
Hemangini Bari

Acquisition Editor
Reshma Raman

Production Coordinator
Arvindkumar Gupta

Content Development Editor
Akashdeep Kundu

Cover Work
Arvindkumar Gupta

Technical Editor
Rohit Kumar Singh

Copy Editors
Roshni Banerjee
Adithi Shetty

About the Author

David Alexander Lillis is an experienced researcher and statistician, having worked in research evaluation, agricultural and forestry statistics, and education research and statistics. Currently, David delivers lectures in mathematics, statistics, and research methods at the New Zealand Institute of Sport in New Zealand. He is the owner and Director of Sigma Statistics and Research Limited, a New Zealand-based consultancy specializing in training, software development, data analysis, and statistical modelling using R. David holds an Honor's degree and Master's degree in Physics and Mathematics, and a PhD from Curtin University in Perth, Australia.

I wish to thank my family — Anna (my wife), David (my eight-year old son), and Coral (my mother) for their patience and support while I worked on this book. In addition, I wish to thank the three reviewers for their helpful feedback.

About the Reviewers

Mzabalazo Z. Ngwenya has worked extensively in the field of statistical consulting and currently works as a biometrician. He holds an MSc degree in Mathematical Statistics from the University of Cape Town, and is currently pursuing a PhD. His research interests include statistical computing, machine learning, and spatial statistics. Previously, he was involved in reviewing *Learning RStudio for R Statistical Computing, Mark P.J. van der Loo and Edwin de Jonge, Packt Publishing*; *R Statistical Application Development by Example Beginner's Guide, Prabhanjan Narayanachar Tattar, Packt Publishing*; and *Machine Learning with R, Brett Lantz, Packt Publishing*.

Donato Teutonico has several years of experience in the modeling and simulation of drug effects and clinical trials in industrial and academic settings. He received his Pharm.D. degree from the University of Turin, Italy, specializing in Chemical and Pharmaceutical Technology, and his PhD in Pharmaceutical Sciences from Paris-Sud University, France.

He is the author of two R packages for Pharmacometrics: CTS template and panels-for-pharmacometrics; both are available on Google code. He is also the author of *Instant R Starter, Packt Publishing*.

Tengfei Yin earned his BS degree in Biological Science and Biotechnology from Nankai University in China and a PhD in Molecular, Cellular and Developmental Biology (MCDB) with a focus on computational biology and bioinformatics from Iowa State University. His research interests include information visualization, high-throughput biological data analysis, data mining, machine learning, and applied statistical genetics. He has developed and maintained several software packages in R and Bioconductor.

www.PacktPub.com

Support files, eBooks, discount offers, and more

You might want to visit www.PacktPub.com for support files and downloads related to your book.

Did you know that Packt offers eBook versions of every book published, with PDF and ePub files available? You can upgrade to the eBook version at www.PacktPub.com and as a print book customer, you are entitled to a discount on the eBook copy. Get in touch with us at service@packtpub.com for more details.

At www.PacktPub.com, you can also read a collection of free technical articles, sign up for a range of free newsletters and receive exclusive discounts and offers on Packt books and eBooks.

http://PacktLib.PacktPub.com

Do you need instant solutions to your IT questions? PacktLib is Packt's online digital book library. Here, you can access, read and search across Packt's entire library of books.

Why subscribe?

- Fully searchable across every book published by Packt
- Copy and paste, print and bookmark content
- On demand and accessible via web browser

Free access for Packt account holders

If you have an account with Packt at www.PacktPub.com, you can use this to access PacktLib today and view nine entirely free books. Simply use your login credentials for immediate access.

Table of Contents

Preface

Reading this book will enable you to learn very quickly how to create wonderful graphics using R. Since R is based on syntax, the time required to master R can be considerable. However, creating high quality and attractive graphics is made easy through the syntax and step-by-step explanations of this book. By reading this book, you will learn how to introduce attractive color schemes, create headings and legends, design your own axes and axes labels, create mathematical expressions on your graphs, and much more.

What this book covers

Chapter 1, *Base Graphics in R – One Step at a Time*, introduces the basic components of a graph (headings, symbols, lines, colors, axes, labels, legends, and so on) and outlines how to use the R syntax to create these components.

Chapter 2, *Advanced Functions in Base Graphics*, covers the techniques required to create professional-level graphs in R, including bar charts, histograms, boxplots, pie charts, and dotcharts. It also covers regression lines, smoothers, and error bars.

Chapter 3, *Mastering the qplot Function*, explains how to use qplot to create a wide range of basic but attractive graphs.

Chapter 4, *Creating Graphs with ggplot*, introduces you to ggplot, which is an even more powerful graphics tool than qplot. We focus on the main techniques to modify your plotting background, titles, grid lines, legends, axes, labels, and colors. It also covers the essential methods to create plots using ggplot. You will learn how to create all the graph types that were covered in *Chapter 1*, *Base Graphics in R – One Step at a Time*, and *Chapter 2*, *Advanced Functions in Base Graphics*, but this time using the many special and attractive features of ggplot.

What you need for this book

To make the most of this book, you need to install R. Go to http://cran.r-project. org/ and click on the relevant download link for either Linux, Mac, or Windows. You will also need to install a plotting package called ggplot2. You can do so within R by entering the following syntax on the command line:

```
install.packages("ggplot2")
```

Who this book is for

If you are a senior undergraduate or postgraduate student, professional researcher, statistician, or analyst, this is the book for you. It is preferable for you to have some prior experience in R. However, even if you are new to R, you can pick up enough from this book to create publication-quality graphs.

Conventions

In this book, you will find a number of styles of text that distinguish between different kinds of information. Here are some examples of these styles, and an explanation of their meaning.

Code words in text, database table names, folder names, filenames, file extensions, pathnames, dummy URLs, user input, and Twitter handles are shown as follows: "The legend() command is very powerful and provides many options to create and place legends."

Any command-line input or output is written as follows:

```
qplot(HEIGHT, WEIGHT_1, data = T, main = "HEIGHT vs. WEIGHT", xlab =
   "HEIGHT (cm)", ylab = "WEIGHT BEFORE TREATMENT (kg)" , geom = "point"
    , colour = factor(ETH), size = 2, alpha = I(0.7))
```

New terms and **important words** are shown in bold. Words that you see on the screen, in menus or dialog boxes for example, appear in the text like this: "Note the use of the **assigns** operator, which consists of the less than sign followed by a minus sign."

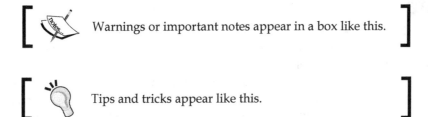

[Warnings or important notes appear in a box like this.]

[Tips and tricks appear like this.]

Reader feedback

Feedback from our readers is always welcome. Let us know what you think about this book—what you liked or may have disliked. Reader feedback is important for us to develop titles that you really get the most out of.

To send us general feedback, simply send an e-mail to feedback@packtpub.com, and mention the book title via the subject of your message.

If there is a topic that you have expertise in and you are interested in either writing or contributing to a book, see our author guide on www.packtpub.com/authors.

Customer support

Now that you are the proud owner of a Packt book, we have a number of things to help you to get the most from your purchase.

Downloading the example code

You can download the example code files for all Packt books you have purchased from your account at http://www.packtpub.com. If you purchased this book elsewhere, you can visit http://www.packtpub.com/support and register to have the files e-mailed directly to you.

Downloading the color images of this book

We also provide you a PDF file that has color images of the screenshots/diagrams used in this book. The color images will help you better understand the changes in the output. You can download this file from: https://www.packtpub.com/sites/default/files/downloads/4553OS_ColorGraphics.pdf.

Errata

Although we have taken every care to ensure the accuracy of our content, mistakes do happen. If you find a mistake in one of our books—maybe a mistake in the text or the code—we would be grateful if you would report this to us. By doing so, you can save other readers from frustration and help us improve subsequent versions of this book. If you find any errata, please report them by visiting http://www.packtpub.com/submit-errata, selecting your book, clicking on the **errata submission form** link, and entering the details of your errata. Once your errata are verified, your submission will be accepted and the errata will be uploaded on our website, or added to any list of existing errata, under the Errata section of that title. Any existing errata can be viewed by selecting your title from http://www.packtpub.com/support.

Piracy

Piracy of copyright material on the Internet is an ongoing problem across all media. At Packt, we take the protection of our copyright and licenses very seriously. If you come across any illegal copies of our works, in any form, on the Internet, please provide us with the location address or website name immediately so that we can pursue a remedy.

Please contact us at copyright@packtpub.com with a link to the suspected pirated material.

We appreciate your help in protecting our authors, and our ability to bring you valuable content.

Questions

You can contact us at questions@packtpub.com if you are having a problem with any aspect of the book, and we will do our best to address it.

1
Base Graphics in R – One Step at a Time

The goal of this chapter is to give you a comprehensive introduction to base graphics in R. By base graphics, I mean graphics created in R without the use of any additional software or contributed packages. In other words, for the time being, we are using only the default packages in R. After reading this chapter, you should be able to create some nice graphs. Therefore, in this chapter I will introduce you to the basic syntax and techniques used to create and save scatterplots and line plots, though many of the techniques here will be useful for other kinds of graph. We will begin with some basic graphs and then work our way to more complex graphs that include several lines and have axes and axis labels of your choice.

In this chapter, we will cover the following topics:

- Basic graphics methods and syntax
- Creating scatterplots and line plots
- Creating special axes
- Adding text—legends, titles, and axis labels
- Adding lines—interpolation lines, regression lines, and curves
- Graphing several variables, multiple plots, and multiple axes
- Saving your graphs as PDF, PostScript, JPG files, and so on
- Including mathematical expressions in your graphs

Learning basic graphics techniques

In R, we create graphs in steps, where each line of syntax introduces new attributes to our graph. In R, we have high-level plotting functions that create a complete graph such as a bar chart, pie chart, or histogram. We also have low-level plotting functions that add some attributes such as a title, an axis label, or a regression line. We begin with the `plot()` command (a high-level function), which allows us to customize our graphs through a series of arguments that you include within the parentheses. In the first example, we start by setting up a sequence of x values for the horizontal axis, running from -4 to +4, in steps of 0.2. Then, we create a quadratic function (y) which we will plot against the sequence of x values.

Enter the following syntax on the R command line by copying and pasting into R. Note the use of the **assigns** operator, which consists of the less than sign followed by a minus sign. In R, we tend to use this operator in preference to the equals sign, which we tend to reserve for logical equality.

```
x <- seq(-4, 4, 0.2)
```

```
y <- 2*x^2 + 4*x - 7
```

Downloading the example code

You can download the example code files for all Packt books you have purchased from your account at http://www.packtpub.com. If you purchased this book elsewhere, you can visit http://www.packtpub.com/support and register to have the files e-mailed directly to you.

You can enter x and y at the command line to see the values that R has created for us.

Now use the `plot()` command. This command is very powerful and provides a range of arguments that we can use to control our plot. Using this command, we can control symbol type and size, line type and thickness, color, and other attributes.

Now enter the following command:

```
plot(x, y)
```

You will get the following graph:

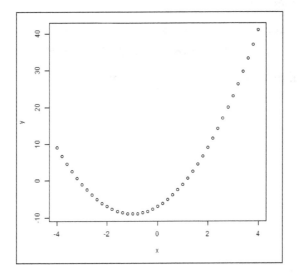

This is a very basic plot, but we can do much better. Let's start again and build a nice plot in steps. Enter the following command, which consists of the `plot ()` command and two arguments:

```
plot(x, y, pch = 16, col = "red")
```

The argument `pch` controls symbol type. The symbol type `16` gives solid dots. A very wide range of colors is available in R and are discussed later in this chapter. The list of available options for symbol type is given in many online sources, but the Quick-R website (`http://www.statmethods.net/advgraphs/parameters.html`) is particularly helpful. Using the previous command, you will get the following graph:

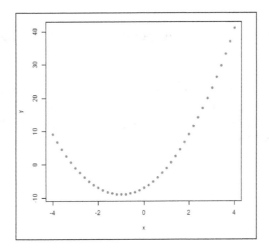

Now we use the arguments `xlim`, `ylim`, `xlab`, and `ylab`. Enter the following plotting syntax on the command line:

```
plot(x, y, pch = 16, col = "red", xlim = c(-8, 8), ylim = c(-20, 50),
main = "MY PLOT", xlab = "X VARIABLE" , ylab = "Y VARIABLE")
```

This command will produce the following graph:

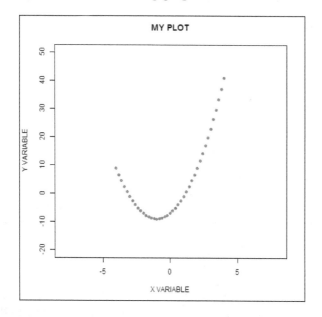

The arguments `xlim` and `ylim` control the axis limits. They are used with the `c` operator to set up the minimum and maximum values for the axes. The arguments `xlab` and `ylab` let you create labels, but you must include your labels within quotation marks.

Now, create line segments between the points using the following command:

```
lines(x, y)
```

Note that the `lines()` command is used after the `plot()` command. It will run provided that the graph produced by the `plot()` command remains open. Next, we will use the `abline()` command, where `abline(a, b)` draws a line of intercept `a` and slope `b`. The commands `abline(h = k)` and `abline(v = k)` draw a horizontal line at the value `k` and a vertical line at the value `k`.

We enter each of these commands on a new line as shown:

```
abline(h = 0)
```

```
abline(v = 0)
```

```
abline(-10, 2)        # Draws a line of intercept -10 and slope 2.
```

```
text(4, 20, "TEXT")
```

```
legend(-8,36,"This is my Legend")
```

Your legend begins at the point (-8, 36) and is now centered on the point (-4, 36). The text() command will be discussed in more detail in *Chapter 2, Advanced Functions in Base Graphics*. The legend() command is very powerful and provides many options for creating and placing legends; it is also discussed in *Chapter 2, Advanced Functions in Base Graphics*. For now, it is enough to know that you specify the position of your legend by entering relevant coordinates as the first two arguments, and then enter your text inside quotation marks.

Consider the following command:

```
rug(x)
```

The rug() command indicates the location of points on the horizontal axis. Here is the resulting graph:

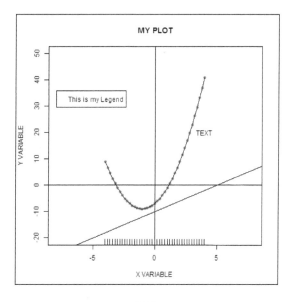

In just a few lines of syntax, you have learned how to make a fairly complex graph and you can now use the same techniques to draw your own graphs.

Creating and joining points

Now, let's look at graphing individual points and creating lines that join them. We start off with a simple plot that has four points. We use the plot() command and group the *x* coordinates together and the *y* coordinates together. To do this job, we use the c operator to combine the *x* values and *y* values independently. Both groups of coordinates are written within parentheses, inside the plot() command. Enter the following syntax on the command line to create a graph with four points:

```
plot(c(1, 2, 3, 6), c(1, 2.5, 3.8, 9.2), pch = 16)
```

This command gives the following plot:

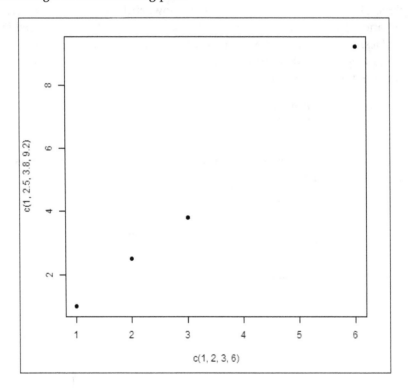

Note how the elements of the first vector gave the horizontal axis values, while the elements of the second vector gave the vertical axis values. Now, we join the four points using the `lines()` command, again grouping the horizontal axis values together and the vertical axis values together:

```
lines(c(1, 2, 3, 6), c(1, 2.5, 3.8, 9.2))
```

The following is the resulting graph, in which the points are now connected by line segments:

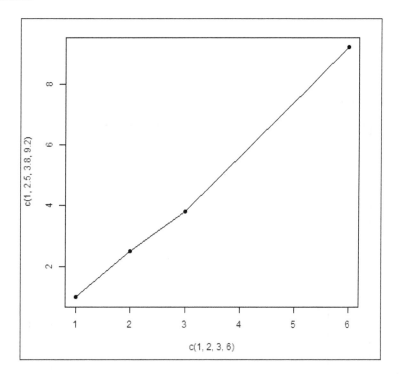

When you encounter plotting commands and arguments and want to know more about them, on the R command line, enter a question mark followed immediately by the command name (for example, `?plot()`) and you will be taken directly to an online help page. You can also try several online resources. One of the best is the Quick-R website (`http://statmethods.net/`), which I mentioned earlier. Go straight to the *Basic Graphs* and *Advanced Graphs* pages. These pages give you a very helpful summary of the main plotting parameters (symbol types, line types, and parameters that control axes, titles, labels, and legends).

Alternatively, you can use a sensible web search (for example, enter R graphs in Google) and you will find several options.

Creating scatterplots and line plots

We have just created a basic graph, but we need more practice. Let's create another plot using the `plot()` command. First we set up a vector of horizontal axis values called **X**, and then a vector of vertical axis values called **Y**. Enter the following syntax on the command line:

```
X <- c(1, 2, 3, 4, 5, 6, 7, 8)
```

```
Y <- c(2, 6, 7, 10, 17, 19, 23, 29)
```

Now let's graph Y against X.

```
plot(X, Y, pch = 16)
```

You'll get the following graph:

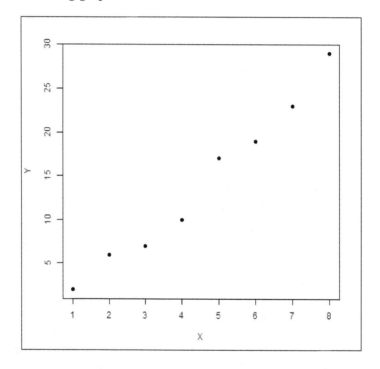

That was simple! However, our graph is very basic. Note that R has decided to create axis ticks every five units on the Y axis. Also, note that if you don't provide horizontal axis values (an *x* axis), by default R will plot your values against a running index.

Let's start again and enhance the graph. Now, we will plot Y using red points using the following command:

```
plot(X, Y, type = "o", col = "red", xlab = "MY X LABEL", ylab = "MY Y
    LABEL")
```

The argument `type="o"` produces symbols joined by straight lines. Now, let's create a title using the `title()` command and the arguments `font.main` and `col.main` to control the title font and colors.

```
title(main = "PLOT 3", font.main = 2, col.main = "blue")
```

Let's look at our graph.

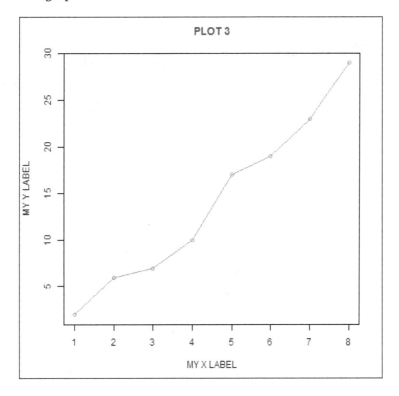

As expected, we have created a title in blue and joined each point with a red line segment.

The font number is an integer between 1 and 5, where 1 is plain, 2 is bold, 3 is italic, 4 is bold italic, and 5 is symbol.

Notice how to create a title. The following are the main font options for graphs:

- `font.axis`: This option specifies the font for the axis annotations
- `font.lab`: This option specifies the font for the axis labels
- `font.main`: This option specifies the font for the (main) title
- `font.sub`: This option specifies the font for a subtitle

Colors in R

To see the range of colors that are available in R, enter the following command:

```
colors()
```

You will see a set (a vector) of 657 colors arranged in alphabetical order. Let's see what we have at various indices in the vector of colors. Enter the following code. It contains square brackets, which allow us to identify and include elements of a vector that has the desired indices.

```
colors()[c(443,109,635, 548, 201)]
```

The output you will get is as follows:

```
1] "lightyellow" "darkslategray1" "turquoise" "purple1" "gray48"
```

 For more details on the available colors in R, refer to `http://research.stowers-institute.org/efg/R/Color/Chart/`.

However, you can control colors very easily using the codes given in the Hexadecimal Color Chart (reproduced from `http://html-color-codes.com/`).

These codes are given as combinations of numerals and alphabetic characters, always starting with the hash symbol (for example, #FF9966, which is a light orange color, or #669933, which is a light olive color). I recommend that you keep a copy of this chart and use the codes to create your own color schemes. You can download it from several sources simply by searching for `Hexadecimal Color Chart`. By referring to this chart, you always know the exact color or hue you are going to get.

© 2000 VisiBone

Passing parameter values to titles and labels

In the next example, we pass parameter values to the title and the axis labels and create the labels using the `paste()` command. This technique can be useful for creating titles and labelling automatically from within an R program (usually called a script). Let's create a set of values first using the following commands:

```
k <- 9
min <- 3
max <- 25
name <- "Mary"
```

Before we start, try the following code:

```
paste(name, "'s Mark", sep = "")
```

You will get the following output:

```
[1] "Mary's Mark"
```

The content of the variable name (`Mary`) was pasted together with the text `'s Mark`. Each element of the text is separated by commas, while the argument `sep = ""` ensures that there are no breaks between the variable and the text. That's the way the `paste()` function works.

Let's start again and enhance the plot. Let's create our plot using colors taken from the Hexadecimal Color Chart. The commands to be used are as follows:

```
plot(X, Y, type="o", col="#669966", xlab = paste(name, "'s Mark",
  sep = ""), ylab = paste("Marks from ", min, " to ", max,  sep =
  ""))
```

Now let's create a title:

```
title(main = paste("Plot ", k, " for ", name, sep = ""),
  font.main = 2, col.main = "#CC6600")
```

The following is our graph, with the appropriate labels and title:

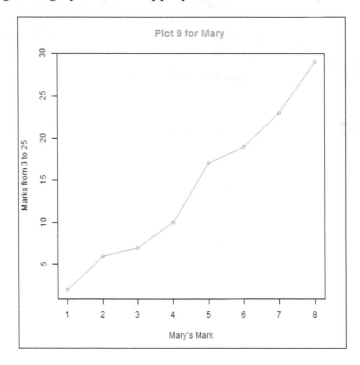

The `title()` command is one way of creating a title. However, by using the `main` argument, you can also create a title within the `plot()` command (as shown in the next example). In the following example, we pass the same parameter values to the title and the axis labels. Enter the following syntax on the command line:

```
plot(X, Y, type = "o", col = "red", main = paste("Plot ", k, " for ",
  name, sep = ""), pch = 16, cex = 1.4, font.main = 2, col.main =
    "blue", xlab = paste(name, "'s Mark", sep = ""), ylab =
      paste("Marks from ", min, " to ", max,  sep = ""))
```

As in the previous example, the `cex` parameter controls the symbol size (the default value is 1). The resulting graph is as follows:

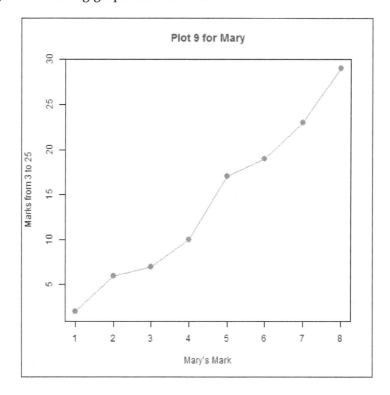

Indeed, we have the correct axis labels and title. You can check out the parameters `pch` and `lty` for yourselves.

Including a regression line

In *Chapter 2, Advanced Functions in Base Graphics*, we will cover **Ordinary Least Squares (OLS)** regressions and plotting regression lines. However, if you are curious as to how to include a regression line, this is how it is done. Use the `abline()` command (which draws lines) in conjunction with the `lm()` command, which performs a regression.

The syntax for performing a regression on the two variables is `lm(Y ~ X)`, where the tilde sign instructs R to perform the regression, with `Y` as the dependent variable and `X` as the independent variable. Now include the following syntax on the command line:

```
abline(lm(Y ~ X))
```

The following is your plot with a regression line:

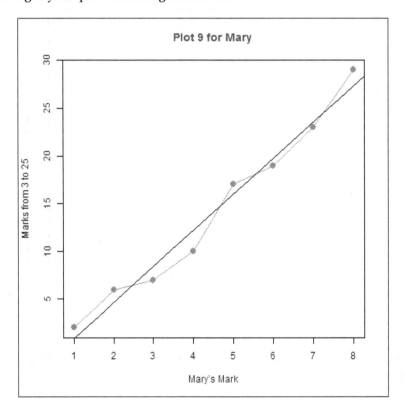

We will cover more about regressions in the next chapter.

Graphing mathematical functions

Sometimes, you may wish to plot a mathematical function. We have already seen how to do that, but the `curve()` command provides a nice alternative. Let's plot a cubic curve using the `curve()` command. To use `curve()`, you must specify a function within the parentheses. Enter the following syntax:

```
curve(5*x**3 + 6*x**2 - 5, -2, 2 , col = "blue", main = "CUBIC
    CURVE")
```

The following is our graph:

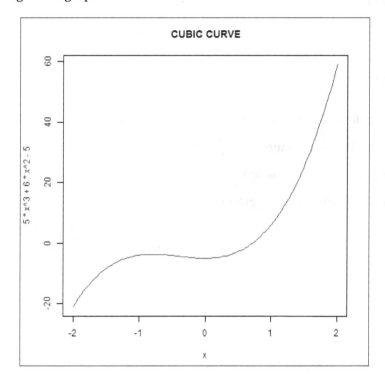

We have a smooth cubic curve and the axis limits we specified within the code. The `curve()` command allows you to specify a function as the first argument, the range of values over which you wish to create your graph, and add your graph to an already existing graph. See the R help function for the `curve()` command by entering `?curve()` on the command line.

R provides many options

Often, R provides several ways to achieve what you want. Let's set up 50 values from -pi to +pi and graph a sine function. We use the seq() command to set up this sequence. Note that R understands the constant Pi, whose value can be obtained using the following command:

```
pi
```

The following output is obtained:

```
[1] 3.141593
```

Now, we create horizontal and vertical axis points for plotting:

```
x <- seq(-pi, pi, length = 50)
y <- sin(x)
```

```
plot(x, y, pch = 17, cex = 0.7, col = "darkgreen")
```

Then, we add a line that connects the points:

```
lines(x, y, col = "darkgreen")
```

Let's take a look at the resulting graph:

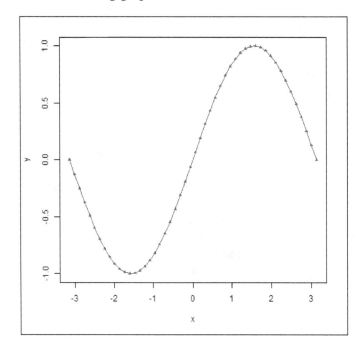

Now try the following approach, using 1000 axis values in order to create a smooth-looking graph:

```
x <- seq(-pi, pi, length = 1000)
y <- sin(x)

plot(x, y, type = "l")
```

The output is as follows:

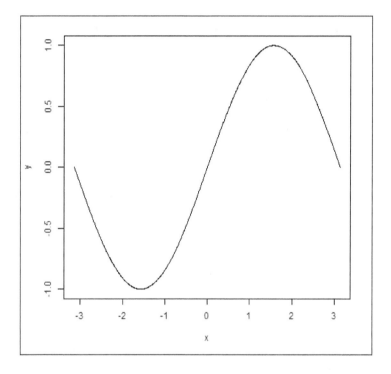

The argument `type = "l"` produces connecting lines, but here we have so many points that the graph appears smooth. Other options include the argument `type = "o"`, which produces symbols joined by straight lines, and `type = "p"`, which produces points.

Creating graphs with several curves

Let's take an example with two dependent variables and create a nice graph. Enter the following code:

```
X   <- c(1, 2, 3, 4, 5, 6, 7)
Y1 <- c(2, 4, 5, 7, 12, 14, 16)
Y2 <- c(3, 6, 7, 8, 9, 11, 12)
```

Now, we graph **Y1** using a vertical axis from 0 to 20 as follows:

```
plot(X, Y1, type="o", pch = 17, cex=1.2, col="darkgreen", ylim=c(0,
    20))
```

Now superpose **Y2** using the following command:

```
lines(Y2, type="o", pch=16, lty=2, col="blue")
```

Notice how we plotted the first curve and then added the second using the `lines()` command. Let's create a title using the `title()` command:

```
title(main="A PLOT OF TWO VARIABLES", col.main="red", font.main=2)
```

Our graph contains two curves, each with the specified line type and symbols:

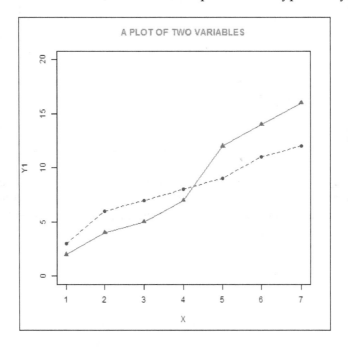

Note the default labels for the horizontal and vertical axes.

Customizing your axes

In R, you can create your own designer axes. The following is another example in which we create designer axes and calculate the vertical axis limits. Let's define three vectors:

```
Y1 <- c(2, 4, 5, 7, 12, 14, 16)
Y2 <- c(3, 6, 7, 8, 9, 11, 12)
Y3 <- c(1, 7, 3, 2, 2, 7, 9)
```

Now, we calculate the maximum value of Y1, Y2, and Y3. Performing this calculation helps us to set the axis limits before we start. Otherwise, the first vector you plot will set the default axis limits, but any other data you read may exceed those limits. The syntax to find the maximum value from the three vectors is as follows:

```
yaxismax <- max(Y1, Y2, Y3)
```

Let's see what the maximum value really is using the following command:

```
yaxismax
```

The output is as follows:

```
[1] 16
```

We want to plot on a vertical axis from 0 to yaxismax. First, we disable the default axes and their annotations, using the arguments axes = FALSE and ann=FALSE, so that we can create our own axes. The approach of disabling the default axes is very important when creating graphs in R.

The argument axes=FALSE suppresses both x and y axes. The arguments xaxt="n" and yaxt="n" suppress the x and y axes individually. The argument ann = FALSE suppresses the axis labels. Now enter the following code:

```
plot(Y1, pch = 15, type="o", col="blue", ylim=c(0, yaxismax),
axes=FALSE, ann=FALSE)


axis(1, at=1:7, lab=c("A","B","C","D","E","F","G"))
```

What does our graph look like at this stage? It looks like this:

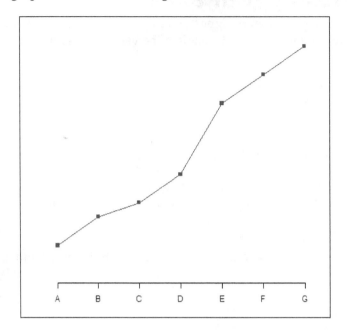

Clearly, we still have work to do to complete the graph by including a vertical axis and title. In the following sections, we will learn how to complete our graph.

Creating axis labels

The first argument in the axis() command (the number 1) specifies the horizontal axis. The at argument allows you to specify where to place the axis labels. The vector called lab stores the actual labels. Now we create a *y* axis with horizontal labels, and ticks every four units, using the syntax at=4*0: yaxismax as shown:

```
axis(2, las=1, at=4*0: yaxismax)
```

Now what does our graph look like?

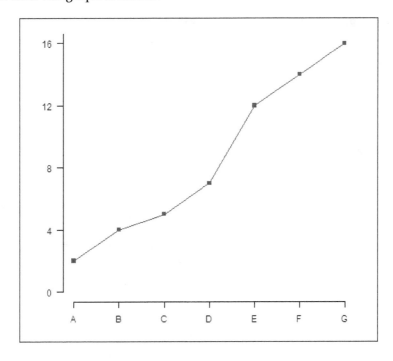

Now we have included a vertical axis. The argument `las` controls the orientation of the axis labels. Your labels can be either parallel (`las=0`) or perpendicular (`las=2`) to your axis. Using `las=1` ensures horizontal labels, while `las=3` ensures vertical labels.

Now we create a box around the plot and then we add in the two new curves using the `lines()` command, using two different symbol types.

```
box()
```

```
lines(Y2, pch = 16, type="o", lty=2, col="red")
```

```
lines(Y3, pch = 17, type="o", lty=3, col="darkgreen")
```

Let's create a title using the following command:

```
title(main="SEVERAL LINE PLOTS", col.main="darkgreen", font.main=2)
```

Now we label the *x* and *y* axes using `title()`, along with `xlab` and `ylab`.

```
title(xlab=toupper("Letters"), col.lab="purple")
```

```
title(ylab="Values", col.lab="brown")
```

Note the `toupper()` command, which always ensures that text within parentheses is uppercase. The `tolower()` command ensures that your text is lowercase.

Finally, we create a legend at the location (`1, yaxismax`), though the `legend()` command allows us to position the legend anywhere on the graph (see *Chapter 2, Advanced Functions in Base Graphics,* for more detail). We include the legend keys using the c operator. We control the colors using `col` and ensure that the symbol types match those of the graph using `pch`. To do this job, we include the legend colors in the same logical order in which we created the curves:

```
legend(1, yaxismax, c("Y1","Y2", "Y3"), cex=0.7, col=c("blue", "red",
    "darkgreen"), pch=c(15, 16, 17), lty=1:3)
```

The following is our final plot:

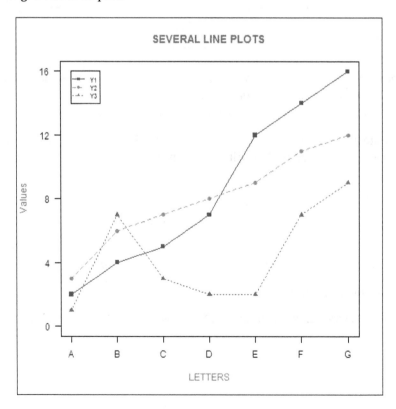

Creating multiple graphs on the same page

You can create multiple plots on the same page (plotting environment) using the command `par(mfrow=(m, n))`, where m is the number of rows and n is the number of columns. Enter the following four vectors:

```
X  <- c(1, 2, 3, 4, 5, 6, 7)
Y1 <- c(2, 4, 5, 7, 12, 14, 16)
Y2 <- c(3, 6, 7, 8, 9, 11, 12)
Y3 <- c(1, 7, 3, 2, 2, 7, 9)
```

In this example, we set the plotting environment at two rows and two columns in order to produce four graphs together:

```
par(mfrow=c(2,2))
```

```
plot(X,Y1, pch = 1)
plot(X,Y2, pch = 2)
plot(X,Y2, pch = 15)
plot(X,Y3, pch = 16)
```

Here is the resulting graph:

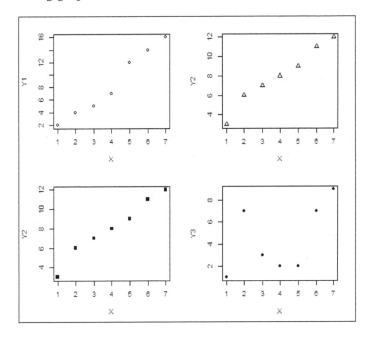

As expected, we have four graphs arranged in two rows and two columns.

Of course, you can vary the number of graphs by setting different numbers of rows and columns.

Saving your graphs

Of course, you will need to save many of the graphs that you create. The simplest method is to click inside the graph and then copy as a metafile or copy as a bitmap. You can then save your graph in a Word document or within a PowerPoint presentation. However, you may wish to save your graphs as JPEGS, PDFs, or in other formats.

Now we shall create a PDF of a graph (a histogram that we will create using the `hist()` command, which you will come across later in this book). First we get ready to create a PDF (in R, we refer to this procedure as opening the PDF device driver) using the command `pdf()`, and then we plot. Finally, we complete the job (closing the device driver) using the command `dev.off()`.

You may wish to save your plot to a particular directory or folder. To do so, navigate to **File** | **Change Dir** in R and select the directory or folder that you wish to use as your R working directory. For example, I selected a directory called BOOK, which is located within the following filepath on my computer:

```
C:\Users\David\Documents\BOOK
```

To confirm that this folder is now my current working folder, I entered the following command:

```
getwd()
```

The output obtained is as follows:

```
[1] "C:/Users/David/Documents/BOOK"
```

R has confirmed that its working folder is the one that I wanted. Note that R uses forward slashes for filepaths. Now, we create a vector of data and create our histogram as follows:

```
y <- c(7, 18, 5, 13, 6, 17, 7, 18, 28, 7,17,28)

pdf("My_Histogram.pdf")
hist(y, col = "darkgreen")
dev.off()
```

A PDF of your histogram should be saved in your R working directory. It is called `My_Histogram.pdf` and it looks like the following:

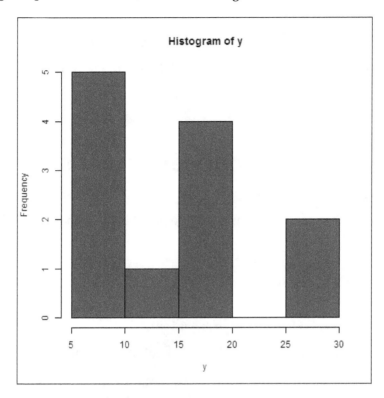

The graphing options available in R include `postscript()`, `pdf()`, `bitmap()`, and `jpeg()`. For a complete list of options, navigate to **Help | Search help** and enter the word `devices`. The list you need is labelled `List of graphical devices`.

For example, to create a postscript plot of the histogram, you can use the following syntax:

```
postscript(file="myplot.ps")
hist(y, col = "darkgreen")
dev.off()
```

To create and save a JPEG image from the current graph, use the `dev.copy()` command:

```
dev.copy(device=jpeg,file="picture.jpg")
dev.off()
```

Your image is saved in the R working directory.

You can save and recall a plot that is currently displayed on your screen. If you have a plot on your screen, then try the following commands:

```
x = recordPlot()
x
```

You can delete your plot but get it back again later in your session using the following command:

```
replayPlot(x)
```

Including mathematical expressions on your plots

Mathematical expressions on graphs are made possible through a combination of two commands, `expression()` and `paste()`, and also through the `substitute()` command.

By itself, the `expression()` command allows you to include mathematical symbols. For example, consider the following syntax:

```
plot(c(1,2,3), c(2,4,9), xlab = expression(phi))
```

This will create a small plot with the Greek symbol phi as the horizontal axis label.

The combination of `expression()` and `paste()` allows you to include mathematical symbols on your graph, along with letters, text, or numerals. Its syntax is `expression(paste())`. Where necessary (that is, where you need mathematical expressions as axis labels), you can switch off the default axes and include Greek symbols by writing them out in English. You can create fractions through the `frac()` command. Note the plus or minus sign, which is achieved though the syntax `%+-%`.

The following is an example based on a similar example in the excellent book *Statistics: An Introduction using R, Michael J. Crawley, Wiley-Blackwell*. I recommend this book to everyone who uses R — both students and professional researchers alike.

We first create a set of values from −7 to +7 for the horizontal axis. We have 71 such values.

```
x <- seq(-7, 7, len = 71)
```

Now we create interesting x and y axes labels. We will disable the x axis in order to create our own axis.

```
plot(x, cos(x),type="l",xaxt="n", xlab=
   expression(paste("Angle",theta)), ylab=expression("sin "*beta))
```

```
axis(1, at = c(-pi, -pi/2, 0, pi/2, pi),
lab = expression(-alpha, -alpha/2, 0, alpha/2, alpha))
```

We insert mathematical text at appropriate places on the graph:

```
text(-pi,0.5,substitute(sigma^2=="37.8"))
```

```
text(-pi/16, -0.5, expression(paste(frac(gamma*omega,
   sigma*phi*sqrt(3*pi)), " ",
      e^{frac(-(3*x-2*mu)^2, 5*sigma^2)}))))
```

```
text(pi,0,expression(hat(y) %+-% frac(se, alpha)))
```

The resulting graph is as follows:

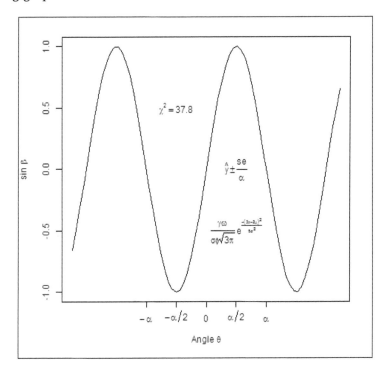

By comparing your own code with that used to produce this graph, you should be able to work out how to create your own mathematical expressions.

Summary

In this chapter, we covered the basic syntax and techniques to produce graphs in R. We covered the essential details for creating scatterplots and line plots, and discussed a range of syntax and techniques that are useful for other kinds of graph. I hope that you found this chapter a useful start on graphing in R.

In the next chapter, we will cover a range of topics that you will need if you want to create professional-level graphs for your own research and analysis. It contains very useful material, so please continue to work through this book by making a start on the next chapter as quickly as possible. For example, in this chapter, though we saw how to draw a regression line, in the next chapter we will go a little further on the topic of graphing regression lines. However, the further chapters have many other interesting techniques for you to learn.

2
Advanced Functions in Base Graphics

The goal of this chapter is to enable you to create different types of graphs in R. In *Chapter 1, Base Graphics in R – One Step at a Time*, you created scatterplots and line plots. Now in this chapter, you will learn how to create other types of graphs, including bar charts, histograms, boxplots, pie charts, and dotcharts. Topics covered in this chapter include the following:

- Including a regression line and residuals in your graph
- Creating complex multiple axes
- Including grid lines and point labels
- Shading and coloring your graph
- Creating bar charts, histograms, boxplots, pie charts, and dotcharts
- Adding LOWESS smoothers to your graph
- Creating scatterplot matrices
- Adding error bars

After working through this chapter, you should understand the principles behind certain advanced plotting functions and should be able to create a wide range of graphs for research and analysis.

Reading datasets into R

Several datasets have been created for this book and can be downloaded from the website for this book as text files. These text files also provide the R code for each chapter. Alternatively, copy the relevant CSV file into a convenient folder, make sure that the R working directory matches your folder, and use the `read.csv()` command. For example, to read a CSV file called `Patients` as the object `T`, enter the following syntax:

```
T <- read.csv("Patients.csv", h=T)
```

Further explanations on reading datasets will be given in this chapter.

Including a regression line and residuals

In the *Creating scatterplots and line plots* section in *Chapter 1, Base Graphics in R – One Step at a Time*, we saw how to use the `abline()` command and the `lm()` command to include a regression line in your graph. Now, we will take this idea a little further. The following regression uses a datafile in which a sample of 10 people rated a film by awarding scores out of 100. These people then viewed the film a second time 1 month later and again awarded scores. We wish to use a regression model to see how well the first rating scores predicted the second rating.

In an OLS regression with one predictor, we fit a model of the following form:

$$Y_i = \beta_0 + \beta_1 X_i + e_i$$

In this form, β_0 is the intercept, β_1 is the slope, and e_i are the errors (or residuals).

Let's perform the regression on the data and plot the results. Along the way, we will learn some useful R syntax. Go to the code file of this chapter, and copy and paste the following syntax into R. It contains the filmrating dataset:

```
filmrating <- structure(list(View1 = c(68L, 47L, 63L, 38L, 60L, 89L,
    42L, 77L, 32L, 67L), View2 = c(85L, 44L, 69L, 38L, 83L, 93L, 35L,
    79L, 91L, 32L)), .Names = c("View1", "View2"), class =
    "data.frame", row.names = c(NA, -10L))
```

Alternatively, you can copy the `Filmratings` CSV file to a folder, match R's working directory to that folder, and use the `read.csv()` function. The argument `h=T` in the following line of code ensures that the column headings are read correctly to the filmrating object:

```
filmrating <- read.csv(Filmratings.csv, h=T)
```

Now, we attach an object using the `attach()` command. Attaching an object is a good idea because R can now identify each variable by name.

```
attach(filmrating)
```

```
filmrating
```

The output is as follows:

```
filmrating
```

	View1	View2
1	68	85
2	47	44
3	63	69
4	38	38
5	60	83
6	89	93
7	42	35
8	77	79
9	32	91
10	67	32

Before we perform the regression, we will plot the two sets of scores. We use the `plot()` command in conjunction with the `main` argument to create headings. We also use the `cex` argument to control the size of data points and axis labels. Enter the following syntax, which consists of the `plot()` command and various arguments with which you are now familiar:

```
plot(View1, View2,pch=16,xlab="First Viewing",ylab="Second Viewing",
  main="FILM RATINGS", cex = 1.5, cex.lab = 1.5, cex.main = 1.6,
    xlim=c(0,100), ylim=c(0,100))
```

Let's look at the resulting graph.

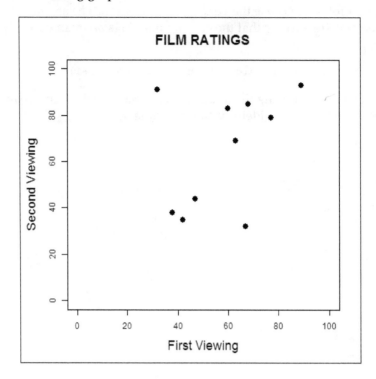

We see that the relationship between the two sets of ratings is not very linear, and a nonlinear model may fit better. However, let's use the lm() command to perform the regression on our data. Since R is object-oriented, we can store the results of the regression as an object, as follows. Let's call the object model.

```
model <- lm(View2 ~ View1)
```

```
model
```

The output you get is as follows:

```
Call:
lm(formula = View2 ~ View1)


Coefficients:
(Intercept)        View1
    32.3066       0.5591
```

We see that the intercept is approximately 32.31 and the slope (the coefficient of the `View1` variable) is approximately 0.56.

Now, we plot the regression line using the `abline()` command as follows:

```
plot(View1, View2,pch=16,xlab="First Viewing",ylab="Second Viewing",
  main="FILM RATINGS", cex = 1.5, cex.lab = 1.5, cex.main = 1.6,
    xlim=c(0,100), ylim=c(0,100))


abline(lm(View2 ~ View1))
```

Here is your graph:

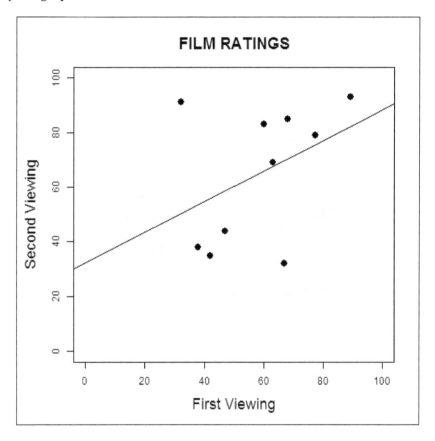

In fact, you could also have used the following syntax:

```
abline(32.31, 0.56)
```

This syntax is used to draw the regression line, but the approach involving the `lm()` command that we used is more concise.

As an exercise, let's draw the residuals (the lines connecting the fitted data with the observed data). We use the `predict()` command to set up the predicted values of the regression model as a new object called `regmodel`. Enter the following syntax, which consists of the `predict()` command and the `lm()` command together:

```
regmodel <- predict(lm(View2 ~ View1))
regmodel
```

The output is as follows:

```
       1        2        3        4        5        6        7        8        9       10
70.32291 58.58259 67.52760 53.55102 65.85041 82.06324 55.78727 75.35448 50.19664 69.76385
```

Remember that the `predict()` command gives us the fitted points from the regression.

Now, we can use the output from the `predict()` command to draw the residuals in order to highlight the differences between the observed data and fitted points. We can use a `for` loop to do this job (many online sources describe `for` loops in R very clearly; for example, http://paleocave.sciencesortof.com/2013/03/writing-a-for-loop-in-r/). Let's see how it is done.

```
for(k in 1:10){ lines(c(View1[k], View1[k]), c(View2[k],
   regmodel[k])) }
```

Here is the resulting graph with regression line and residuals:

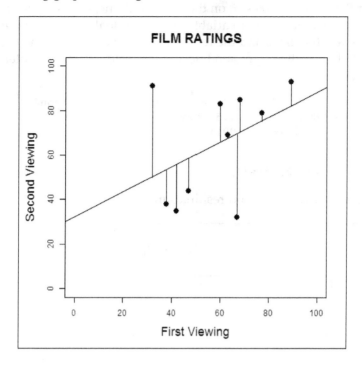

Note the syntax involved in creating the `for` loop. This syntax involves a running index from 1 to the total number of points and the `lines()` command, which connects the observed and fitted data. The observed data consists of points defined by (`View1`, `View2`), while the fitted model values consist of points defined by (`View1`, `regmodel`).

Of course, entering the previous code to draw the residuals is cumbersome, so here is a function that I wrote to do this job efficiently. It is called `drawresid()`. First, you must enter the entire function on the R command line:

```
drawresid <- function(X, Y, col){
  abline(lm(Y ~ X), col = col)
  regressionmodel <- predict(lm(Y ~ X))
  for(k in 1:length(X)){ lines(c(X[k], X[k]), c(Y[k],
    regressionmodel[k]), col = col) } }
```

This function is given in the code file for this chapter. Let's use it on our film scores dataset. Enter the word `drawresid` on the command line, and then, for the three arguments, give the independent variable, the dependent variable, and finally the color of the residual lines and the regression line. To illustrate the use of this function, we will draw the regression line and the residuals in red. Enter all of the following syntax:

```
plot(View1, View2,pch=16,xlab="First Viewing",ylab="Second Viewing",
   main="FILM RATINGS", cex = 1.5, cex.lab = 1.5, cex.main = 1.6,
     xlim=c(0,100), ylim=c(0,100))
```

```
drawresid(View1, View2, "red")
```

The graph with regression line and residuals in red is as follows:

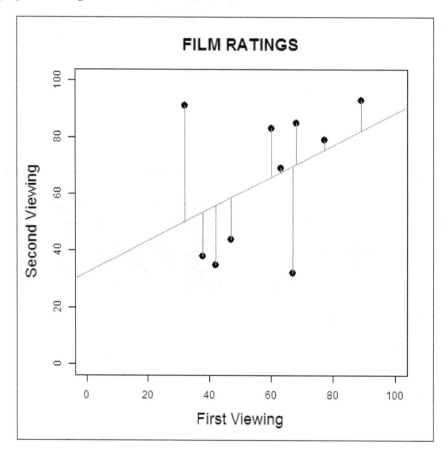

I hope that you find this function useful.

A medical dataset to create graphs

For many of the examples in this book, we will use the following dataset. It gives medical data on 45 people: their names; their gender (a two-level categorical variable); their ethnicity (a four-level categorical variable, labeled 1, 2, and 3); the medical treatment they received (a three-level categorical variable with levels A, B, or C); their age band (a three-level categorical variable with levels Y, M, and E, standing for young, middle-aged, and elderly); their weight (body mass) before treatment (in kg) and weight (body mass) after treatment (in kg), their heights (in cm); whether they smoke (a two-level categorical variable with levels Y and N); whether they perform regular exercise (a two-level categorical variable with levels TRUE and FALSE); and finally, whether or not they recovered after treatment (a two-level categorical variable with levels 1 and 0). We read this dataset as an object called T. The syntax to read this dataset is given in the code file of this chapter. You can either copy and paste it directly from the text file, or save the `Patients.csv` file in a folder and read the data into R using `read.csv()`. Then, use the following command:

```
head(T)
```

We get the following output:

	PATIENT	GENDER	ETH	TREATMENT	AGE	WEIGHT_1	WEIGHT_2	HEIGHT	SMOKE	EXERCISE	RECOVER
1	Mary	F	1	A	Y	79.2	76.6	169	Y	TRUE	1
2	Jim	M	2	B	Y	87.5	84.8	178	Y	TRUE	0
3	Bob	M	2	A	M	65.1	64.6	162	N	FALSE	1
4	Dave	M	1	B	M	58.8	59.3	161	Y	FALSE	0
5	Simon	M	1	C	M	72.0	70.1	175	N	FALSE	1
6	Ben	M	3	A	Y	95.9	94.5	188	N	FALSE	1

Again, we attach an object using the `attach()` command:

```
attach(T)
```

Let's now create a similar regression plot for the height and weight variables of our medical dataset. This job is done using the following syntax:

```
plot(WEIGHT_1, HEIGHT,pch=16,xlab="WEIGHT BEFORE TREATMENT
  (kg)",ylab="HEIGHT (cm)", main="HEIGHT VS. WEIGHT", cex = 0.8,
    cex.lab = 1.5, cex.main = 1.6, xlim=c(0,150), ylim=c(100,200))
```

Here is our graph:

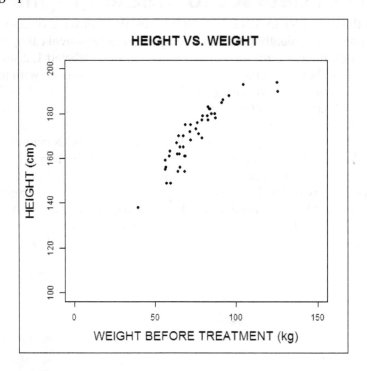

Now, we create the regression model using `lm()`:

```
mod <- lm(HEIGHT ~ WEIGHT_1)
```

```
mod
```

We get the following output:

```
Call:
lm(formula = HEIGHT ~ WEIGHT_1)

Coefficients:
(Intercept)      WEIGHT_1
   119.7836        0.6737
```

The intercept is approximately 119.78 and the slope (the coefficient of the weight variable) is approximately 0.67. It gives the change in height for a weight change of one unit. Now we plot the regression line:

```
abline(lm(HEIGHT ~ WEIGHT_1))
```

The following is the graph with the regression line:

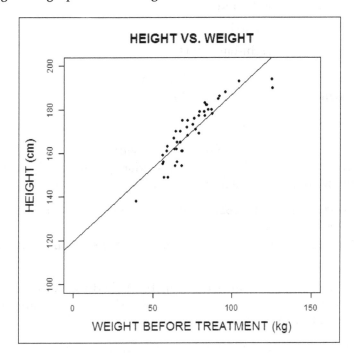

We will not draw the residuals this time, as this graph would look very cluttered if we did. However, by now you should know how to draw both regression lines and residuals.

Creating complex multiple axes

Now we will create a graph with two curves and three axes. First, let's read the following vectors of data:

```
x <- c(-25:25)
```

```
y <- 1.5*x + 2
```

```
z <- 0.3*(x**2) - 20
```

In the preceding code, we have a linear function and a quadratic function. As you will see, we will need some extra room for text on the right-hand margin. This is because we wish to add some explanatory text there. By default, graphs in R have margins that are as follows:

- 5-lines wide on the bottom axis
- 4-lines wide on the left-hand axis
- 4-lines wide on the top axis
- 2-lines wide on the right-hand axis

We want to create a right-hand margin 8.1-lines wide on the right axis using the `mar` argument, which controls margin widths:

```
par(mar=c(5, 4, 4, 8) + 0.1)
```

Note the syntax for changing the default margin width for any axis. You simply insert the desired line width value in the appropriate position within the `mar` argument. Now, we disable the default axes and plot as follows:

```
plot(x, y,type="o", pch=14, col="red", xaxt="n", yaxt="n", lty=3,
  xlab="", ylab="")
title("MY DESIGNER AXES", xlab=" HORIZONTAL AXIS", ylab="VERTICAL
  AXIS")
```

We now include a plot of z (the quadratic function). To do so, let's use line-type b, consisting of both points and lines. Let's also use dashes using the argument `lty = 2`. Use the following syntax:

```
lines(x, z, type="b", pch=16, col="blue", lty=2)
```

Now, we create a horizontal axis in the usual position using the following syntax:

```
axis(1, at=seq(-25,25,5),labels= seq(-25,25,5), col.axis="blue",
  las=2)
```

Now, we create a vertical axis as follows:

```
axis(2, at=seq(-25,25,10),labels= seq(-25,25,10), col.axis="red",
  las=2)
```

Next, we create an axis to the right using `axis (4, . . .)` with value labels at each point. Also, we will use smaller text and tick marks. If we wanted to create an axis at the top of the graph, we would use `axis (3, . . . )` with value labels at each point.

```
axis(4, at=z, labels=round(z,digits=2), col.axis="blue", las=2,
cex.axis=0.5, tck=-.02)
```

The `tck` argument controls the length of the tick marks, setting their length as a fraction of the plotting area. The default value for `tck` is 0.01. Setting `tck = 0` gets rid of tick marks, while setting `tck = 1` creates gridlines. Finally, by including the syntax `cex.axis = 0.5`, we have just set the axis labels to half their default size.

You can add text to your graphs using the `text()` and `mtext()` commands. The `text()` command places text within the graph, while `mtext()` places text in one of the four margins.

```
text(location, "text to include . . . ", pos, ...)
  mtext("text to place", side, line=n, ...)
```

Finally, we include a title for the right-hand axis using `mtext()`:

```
mtext("An axis for z", side=4, line=3, cex.lab=1.3,las=2, col="blue")
```

Now, we see that our graph indeed has three axes and that the right-hand axis tick marks match the data of the quadratic curve:

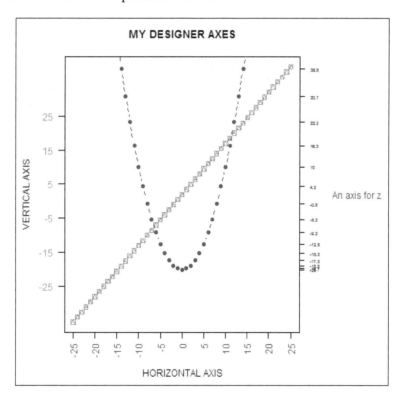

You can use the same techniques to create complex axes for your own graphs.

Superposing graphs

To superpose graphs, the argument add=T can be very useful, but you can use it only when you have an analytic expression for each curve. Here, we plot three exponential functions together using curve():

```
curve(3 * exp(-x/2), from = 0, to = 10, ylim = c(0, 2), ylab = "",
  col = "red", lwd = 2)
```

```
curve(4 * exp(-x), add = T, lty = 4, col = "blue", lwd = 2)
```

```
curve(2.5 * exp(-x/3), add = T, lty = 3, col = "darkgreen", lwd = 2)
```

The syntax ylab = "" ensures that no *y* axis label is created. Now, add text at the right places using expression() and paste(), which we saw at the end of *Chapter 1, Base Graphics in R – One Step at a Time*. You must determine where to place the text by examining the graph carefully.

```
text(3.2, 1.9, expression(paste("My First Exponential: ", 3 * e^(-
  x/2))), col = "red")
text(2.8, 0, expression(paste("My Second Exponential: ", 4 * e^(-
  x))), col = "blue" )
text(7, 0.7, expression(paste("My Third Exponential: ", 2.5 * e^(-
  x/3))), col = "darkgreen" )
```

You should get the following graph:

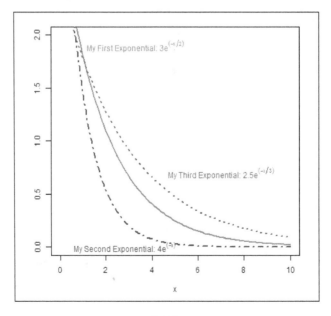

Note that in each case the text is centered on the x value that you provided within the text() command.

Creating point labels

You can use the text() function to label the points on your graph. To do so, you create a set of *x* and *y* coordinates and include the text as a vector of labels. Let's work through the following example. The dataset for this example gives the heights of a group of children of different ages. Again, you can cut and paste this dataset from the code file this chapter or save the Children.csv file and read the data using read.csv(). We will produce a plot of height against age for each child, labeling each point according to the child's name.

```
cheight <-
structure(list(Child = structure(c(4L, 3L, 2L, 1L), .Label =
  c("Anne", "John", "Mary", "Steven"), class = "factor"), Age =
    c(13L, 11L, 12L, 17L), Height = c(165L, 145L, 154L, 157L)),
      .Names = c("Child", "Age", "Height"), class = "data.frame",
        row.names = c(NA, -4L))
```

As done in previous examples, we attach the object to make the variables visible by name using the following command:

```
attach(cheight)
```

First, we create a basic graph as follows:

```
plot(Age, Height, main = "Heights of Four Children at Various Ages",
  pch = 16, ylab = "Height (cm)", xlab = "Age (yrs)" ,ylim = c(140,
    180),xlim = c(10, 18))
```

Then, we add labels to each point. The argument Child (the third argument within the text() function) ensures that the children's names provide a label for each point.

```
text(Age, Height, Child, cex=1.2, pos=3, col="red")
```

Let's examine our graph:

Note that we used the argument `pos = 3` to place the text above each point. You can experiment with the other options: `pos = 1` (below the points), `pos = 2` (to the left), and `pos = 4` (to the right).

Including a grid on your graph

You can add a grid to your plot using the `grid()` command. Let's set up a simple graph and add a grid:

```
x <- seq(1:5)
y <- x
plot(x, y, pch = 16)
```

Let's add a default grid with horizontal and vertical grid lines at major units in both the horizontal and vertical directions:

```
grid()
```

You get the following graph:

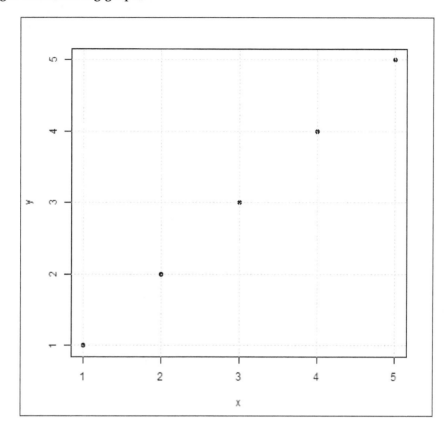

Now, we omit the horizontal grid lines using ny = NA. Of course, you could do the same for the vertical grid lines.

```
plot(x, y, pch = 16)
grid(ny=NA)
```

We get the following graph:

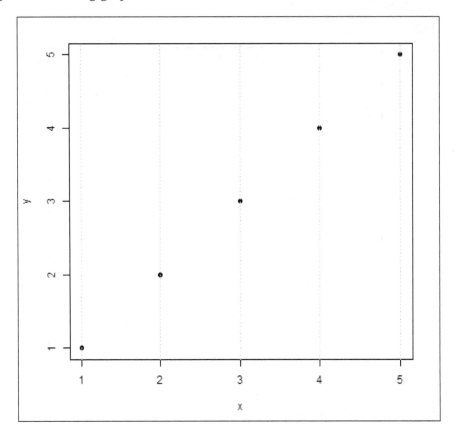

Setting the numbers of grid lines to NULL produces the default option of grid lines at every unit, for example:

```
plot(x, y, pch = 16)
grid(nx = NULL, ny = NULL)
```

Shading and coloring your graph

You can shade and color your graphs using the polygon() command. To use the polygon() command, you must specify the horizontal and vertical axis limits, but you must also include the *x* and *y* variables as the middle arguments.

Let's create a quadratic curve and shade under it with a light green selected from the Hexadecimal Color Chart:

```
x <- 1:100
y <- 3*x^2 + 2*x + 7
plot(x, y)
lines(x, y)


polygon(cbind(c(min(x), x, max(x)), c(min(y), y, min(y))),
  col="#00CC66")
```

Here is the graph:

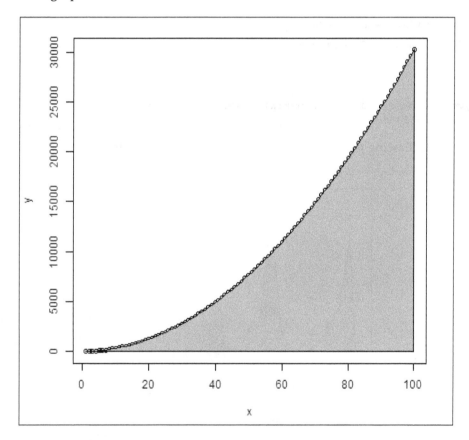

Using this approach, the `polygon()` command shades under the curve, between the minimum and maximum values of the *x* variable and below the *y* variable. The syntax involving `cbind()` is an elegant way of including the relevant limits.

The following example is more complex. It uses the `rnorm()` command to simulate values from a normal distribution, with a given mean and standard deviation. By default, random values with a mean of 0 and a standard deviation of 1 are produced. For example, to select a sample of 30 values from a normal distribution with a mean of 12 and standard deviation of 4, use the following syntax:

```
sample <- rnorm(30, mean=12, sd=4)
```

OK. Let's proceed with the example, this time choosing a nice light brown color from the Hexadecimal Color Chart. For this example, we will select a random sample of 25 from a normal distribution with a mean of two and standard deviation of three and shade under those points:

```
x <- 1:25
y <- rnorm(25, mean=2, sd=3)
plot(x, y, pch = 16, cex=0.8)
lines(x, y)


polygon(cbind(c(min(x), x, max(x)),c(min(y), y, min(y))),
   col="#FF9933")
```

We get the following graph, with light brown coloring below the curve:

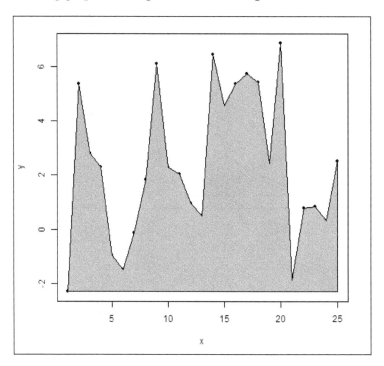

Now we shade above the curve with another attractive color from the Hexadecimal Color Chart:

```
plot(x, y, pch = 16, cex = 0.8)
```

```
lines(x, y)
polygon(cbind(c(min(x), x, max(x)),c(max(y), y, max(y))),
  col="#CC66FF")
```

To shade above the curve, we changed the third argument of the group of y values from minimum y to maximum y. Let's see the graph, with coloring above the curve, which is as follows:

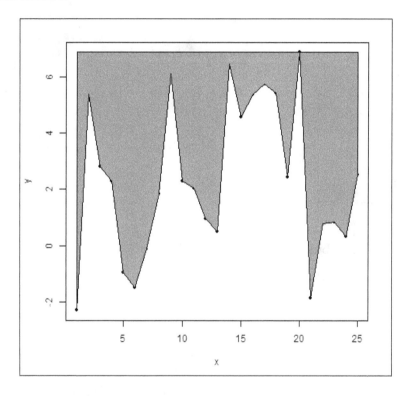

Now let's see how to shade between the curve and the *x* axis.

```
plot(x, y)
```

```
lines(x, y)
```

```
polygon(cbind(c(min(x), x, max(x)), c(0, y, 0)), col="#339966")
```

Here is our graph.

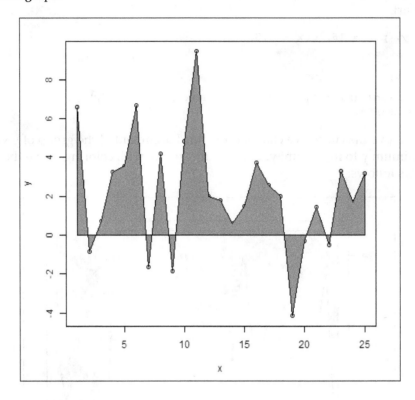

To shade between the curve and the *x* axis, we used zeroes for the first and third vertical axis values. Obviously, you could shade both above and below the curve:

```
plot(x, y, pch = 16, cex = 0.8)


lines(x, y)


polygon(cbind(c(min(x), x, max(x)),c(max(y), y, max(y))),
  col="#66CCCC")
polygon(cbind(c(min(x), x, max(x)),c(min(y), y, min(y))),
  col="#339999")
```

We get this graph:

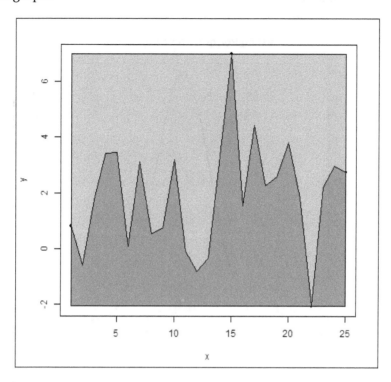

Using polygon() to shade under a normal curve

We will use the dnorm() command to create a standard normal curve and we will use polygon() to shade under the normal curve. The syntax is as follows:

```
dnorm(x, mean = 0, sd = 1)
```

This creates a set of probabilities from a normal probability distribution with a mean of 0 and a standard deviation of 1. Thus, the following syntax creates a normal distribution graph from -5 to 5:

```
x <- seq(-5, 5, length=1000)
y <- dnorm(x)


plot(x, y, type="l", lwd=2, col="blue", xlab="Z Value",
  ylab="Probability", main="Testing Polygon with a Normal Curve")
```

We get the following graph:

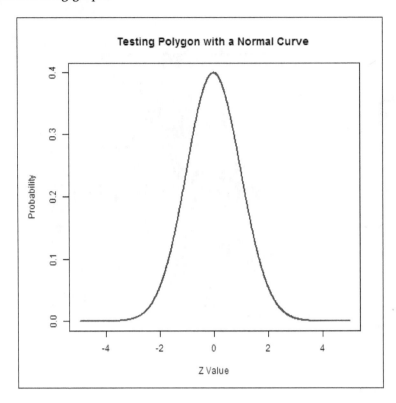

We have plotted the curve using 1000 points in order to give a smooth appearance, but we must create an appropriate set of x and y values for `polygon()`. Let's shade under the entire curve with a pale lemon yellow color from the Hexadecimal Color Chart:

```
plot(x, y, type="l", lwd=2, col="blue", xlab="Z Value",
  ylab="Probability", main="Testing Polygon with a Normal Curve")
```

Finally, we invoke `polygon()` as follows:

```
polygon(c(-5, x, 5), c(0, y, 0), col="#FFFF66")
```

This command will produce the following graph:

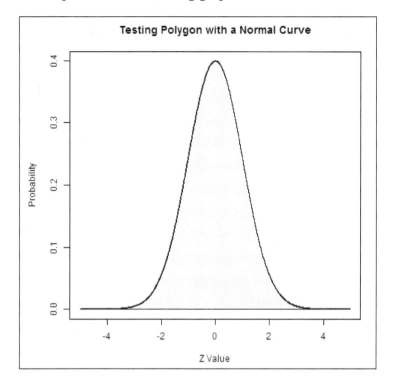

Let's start again and shade between two Z values.

```
plot(x, y, type="l", lwd=2, col="blue", xlab="Z Value",
  ylab="Probability", main="Testing Polygon with a Normal Curve")
```

Next, we create the horizontal axis values. Let's suppose that we wish to shade from the point -3 to -1.5 on the **Z Value** axis, again using a large number of points. We recalculate the probabilities for this set of *x* values.

```
x <- seq(-3, -1.5, length=100)
y <- dnorm (x)
```

Finally, we invoke `polygon()`:

```
polygon(c(-5, x, -1.5), c(0, y, 0), col="#669966")
```

The output graph is as follows:

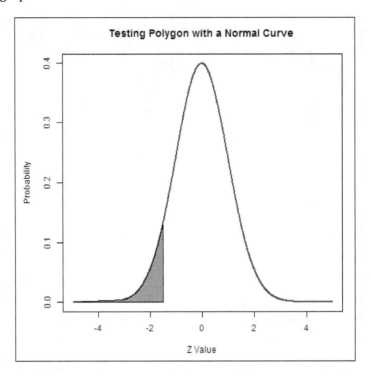

You can use `polygon()` to create many interesting graphs, not only for shading between curves and axes. To develop your skill in using the `polygon()` command, you must read the standard texts and helpful websites and study the worked examples carefully. Additionally, you can enter `?polygon()` on the command line and you will be taken to a web page that explains the `polygon()` command.

Creating bar charts

Let's see how to create bar charts in R. We will create a simple bar chart using the `barplot()` command, which is easy to use. First, we set up a vector of numbers. Then we count them using the `table()` command and plot the counts. The `table()` command creates a simple table of counts of the elements in a dataset. Enter the following vector into R:

```
H <- c(2,3,3,3,4,5,5,5,5,6)
```

Now, we count each element using the `table()` command as follows:

```
counts <- table(H)
counts
```

The output is as follows:

```
H
2 3 4 5 6
1 3 1 4 1
```

Now we plot the counts.

```
barplot(counts)
```

Here is the bar chart:

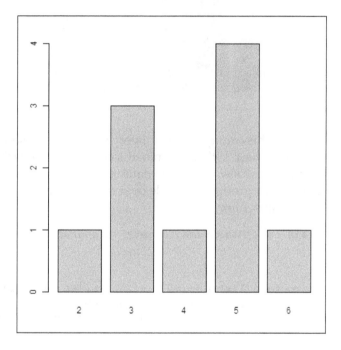

The horizontal axis records the elements in your dataset, while the vertical axis gives the counts of each element. You will see that the `barplot()` command does not perform the count directly, so we used the `table()` command first.

You can plot your data directly if you omit the `table()` command. In that case, the height of the bars will match the actual values of the dataset. This technique is useful if your data are already in the form of counts or if you wish to plot the magnitudes of each element.

```
D <- c(3, 7, 12, 2, 0, 5)

barplot(D, col="blue")
```

The output graph is as follows:

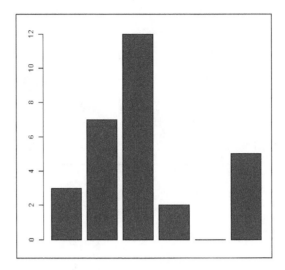

It's that simple! However, this example was not very sophisticated so we will now create a more complex bar chart. Either download the measurements CSV file or cut and paste from the book's website. The dataset consists of a set of medical measurements made on four groups of people over five trials. Next you read the dataset using the following syntax:

```
measurements <- read.csv("Measurements.csv", header=T, sep=",")
```

Or

```
measurements <- structure(list(Group1 = c(1L, 3L, 6L, 4L, 9L), Group2
  = c(2L, 5L, 4L, 5L, 12L), Group3 = c(4L, 4L, 6L, 6L, 16L), Group4 =
    c(3L, 5L, 6L, 7L, 6L)), .Names = c("Group1", "Group2", "Group3",
      "Group4"), class = "data.frame", row.names = c(NA, -5L))
attach(measurements)
```

```
measurements
```

The output is as follows:

	Group1	Group2	Group3	Group4
1	1	2	4	3
2	3	5	4	5
3	6	4	6	6
4	4	5	6	7
5	9	12	16	6

Let's create a bar chart for Group3 with labels.

```
barplot(measurements$Group3, main="Group 3 Measurements",
  xlab="TRIAL", ylab="Measurement",
    names.arg=c("T1","T2","T3","T4","T5"), border="red",
      density=c(90, 70, 50, 40, 30))
```

Here is the graph:

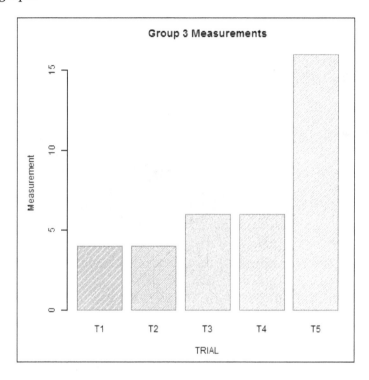

In the preceding graph, we have labeled each trial with an uppercase T followed by the trial number.

What did the density parameter achieve? Try other values of the density parameter and see what you get. The command names.arg enables you to supply your preferred horizontal axis labels.

We will now create another bar chart, this time using R's rainbow palette. We continue to use the measurements dataset of the previous example, but we now wish to graph all of the data. We plot a bar chart with adjacent bars by using the as.matrix() command and the argument beside = T:

```
barplot(as.matrix(measurements), main="ALL MEASUREMENTS", ylab =
  "Measurements", cex.lab = 1.5, cex.main = 1.4, beside=TRUE,
    col=heat.colors(5))
```

The output bar chart is as follows:

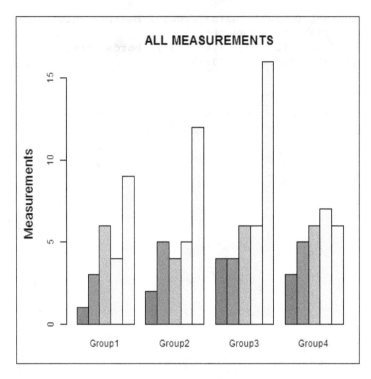

We created an attractive bar chart using `as.matrix()` and the `heat.colours` palette.

Including a legend

In *Chapter 1, Base Graphics in R – One Step at a Time*, we saw how to create a legend. Let's look again at creating legends using the grouped bar chart we discussed in the previous section. Now, we will create a legend at the top-left corner. To create a legend without a frame, we use `bty="n"`. The `bty` argument controls borders. We pass the same color palette to the legend using the `fill` argument.

```
barplot(as.matrix(measurements), main="ALL MEASUREMENTS", ylab =
  "Measurements", cex.lab = 1.5, cex.main = 1.4, beside=TRUE,
    col=heat.colors(5))
```

```
legend("topleft", c("Measure 1","Measure 2","Measure 3","Measure 4",
  "Measure 5"), cex=1.3, bty="n", fill=heat.colors(5))
```

The output is as follows:

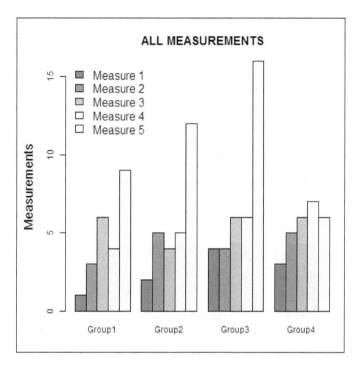

We used the `topleft` argument to position the legend towards the top-left corner of the chart. Other options include the following:

```
"bottomright", "bottom", "bottomleft", "left", "topleft", "top",
  "topright","right", "center".
```

For several of the examples from now on, we will use the medical dataset that you have already met in this chapter. Let's create a horizontal barplot with labels using the `table()` command. We use the TREATMENT variable of the medical dataset, which you must now read again as the object T. Again, either cut and paste the dataset from the website or use the `read.csv()` command on the CSV file.

Now, we will create a table.

```
treatment <- table(TREATMENT)
```

```
treatment
```

The output is as follows:

```
TREATMENT
 A  B  C
16 17 12
```

We set up our colors as a vector:

```
colours <- c("red", "yellow", "blue")
```

```
barplot(treatment, main="Treatment", horiz=TRUE, col= colours,
names.arg=c("A", "B", "C"))
```

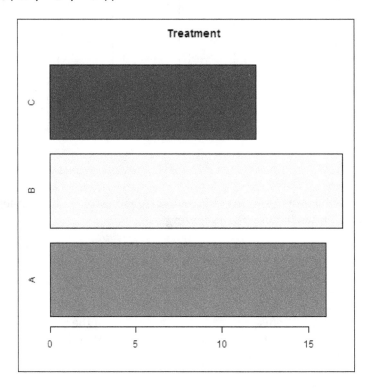

We obtained a horizontal barplot. For a vertical bar chart, we omit the argument `horiz = T`:

```
barplot(treatment, main="Treatment", col= colours,
names.arg=c("A", "B", "C"))
```

The output is as follows:

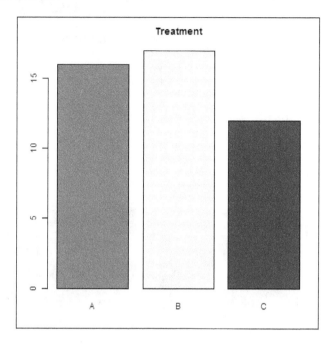

Now, we will create a stacked barplot of numbers of smokers, with nice colors and a legend. To get the stacked barplot, we omit the argument `beside = T`:

```
smoketh <- table(as.numeric(ETH), as.numeric(SMOKE))
smoketh
```

The output is as follows:

```
    SMOKE
ETH N Y
  1 9 3
  2 9 9
  3 7 8
```

Now, we will create the stacked barplot.

```
barplot(smoketh, main="Numbers of Smokers by Ethnicity",
xlab="Non-Smoker or Smoker", ylab ="Number of Smokers",
  col=c("blue","red","yellow"), legend = rownames(smoketh))
```

We get the following output:

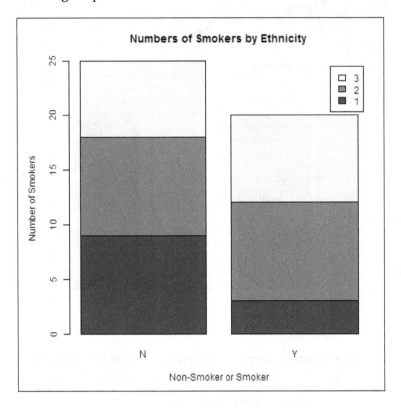

Creating histograms

Now, we will create a histogram for patients' weight after treatment. The data is contained in the WEIGHT_2 variable. Enter the following syntax involving the hist() command:

```
hist(WEIGHT_2)
```

The graph is as follows:

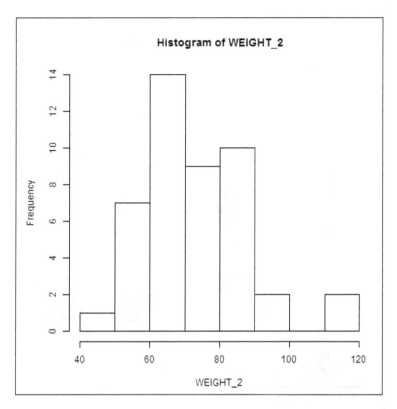

It is easy to create a basic histogram in R. Now, let's create a histogram from all the data in the measurements dataset. First, we transform the four vectors into a single vector and make a histogram of all elements:

```
G <- c(Group1, Group2, Group3, Group4)
```

Finally, we can create a histogram in a nice purple hue from the Hexadecimal Color Chart:

```
hist(G, col="#FF00CC", ylim=c(0,10), main = "HISTOGRAM OF ALL
    MEASUREMENTS", xlab ="MEASURE", ylab ="FREQUENCY")
```

Our histogram is as follows:

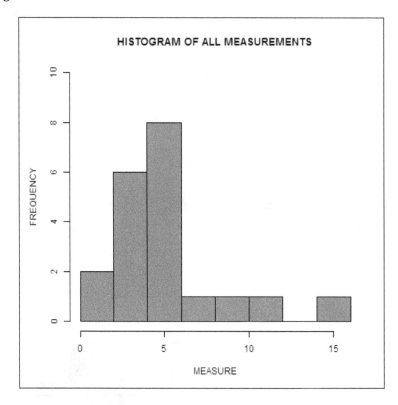

Now, we will create a more complex example using the same dataset. We find the maximum value in order to set the horizontal axis limits:

```
max <- max(G)
max
```

The output is as follows:

```
[1] 16
```

The maximum value is 16. We want a histogram bin for every count, so we set the `breaks` argument equal to the maximum value of the dataset. We use a light gray from the Hexadecimal Color Chart. In addition, we make the horizontal axis labels perpendicular to the axis using `las` = 2. Use the following syntax:

```
hist(G, col= "#CCCCCC", breaks=max, xlim=c(0,max),
main="HISTOGRAM OF MEASUREMENTS", las=2, xlab = "Values", cex.lab =
  1.3)
```

The following bar chart is the output:

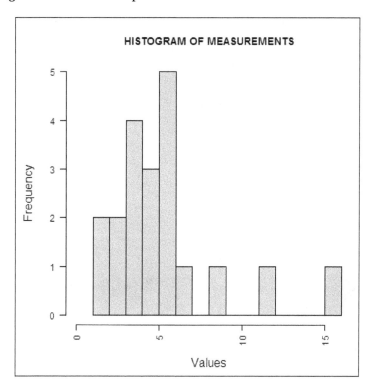

Note the effect of the argument `las=2` and compare it with the effect of `las=1`. Of course, the argument `cex.lab` allowed us to set the size of the labels.

The `hist()` command uses algorithms that calculate the number of bins. Let's try setting the number of bins to six. We use another color from the Hexadecimal Color Chart. Use the following syntax:

```
hist(G, col =  "#FF3366", breaks=6, xlim=c(0,max),

main=" HISTOGRAM OF MEASUREMENTS ", las=2, xlab = "Values", cex.lab =
   1.3)
```

The output is as follows:

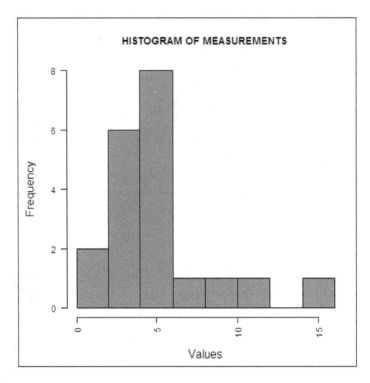

Although we wanted six bins, the `hist()` function has returned eight. However, setting up histogram bins as a vector gives you more control over the number of bins. Now, we will set up the bins as a vector (four bins in total), each bin four units wide. Our vector contains the maximum and minimum values of each bin. Use the following syntax:

```
measurebins <- c(0, 4, 8, 12, 16)

hist(G, col = "#9933CC", breaks=measurebins, xlim=c(0,max),
main=" HISTOGRAM OF MEASUREMENTS ", las=2, xlab = "Values", cex.lab =
    1.3)
```

The output is as follows:

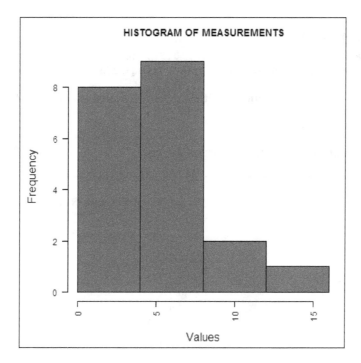

We have produced a histogram with the required number of bins.

Sometimes, it is helpful to fit a normal curve to a histogram. If you want to do so, then use `dnorm()`. To illustrate the approach, we now create a random sample of 50 numbers with a mean of 0 and a standard deviation 1 using the `rnorm()` command:

```
z <- rnorm(50)
```

Enter z on the command line to see your numbers. We must be precise about our lower and upper limits for the horizontal axis. Therefore, we eliminate all values outside four standard deviations from the mean. We use the following command to do this job. We use square brackets to subset Z and we use the less than and greater than comparison operators. We also include a vertical line, which is the operator for logical OR:

```
z[z < -4 | z > 4] <- NA
```

Now, set up a sequence of horizontal axis values from –4 to +4 in steps of 0.1 (for plotting):

```
x <- seq(-4, 4, 0.1)
hist(Z, breaks=seq(-4, 4), ylim=c(0, 0.5), col="red", main =
  "HISTOGRAM WITH FITTED NORMAL CURVE", freq=FALSE)
```

Now the `lines()` command, along with `dnorm()`, creates the normal curve:

```
lines(x, dnorm(x), lwd=2)
```

Here is the histogram with a fitted normal curve:

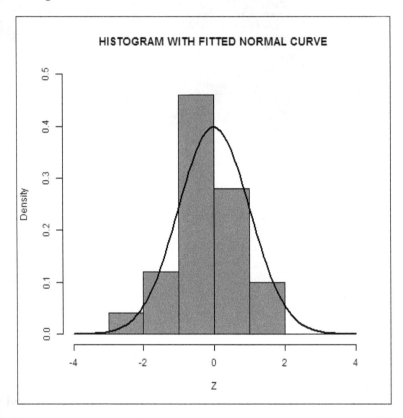

Let's use this technique to fit a histogram of patients' heights and fit a standard normal curve. We standardize the height data by subtracting the mean and dividing by the standard deviation. The `sd()` command returns the standard deviation. Use the following syntax:

```
HSTD <- (HEIGHT - mean(HEIGHT))/ sd(HEIGHT)
```

Now, we set up a sequence of horizontal axis values for plotting. To do so, we examine the range of the standardized data. We use the range() command to do so:

```
range(HSTD)
```

We will get the following output from the range() command:

```
[1] -2.547588  1.883000
```

Our horizontal axis must include these minimum and maximum values, so let's set up a horizontal axis running from -3 to 3:

```
x <- seq(-3, 3, 0.1)
```

Now, we will plot the histogram of the standardized height.

```
hist(HSTD, breaks=seq(-3, 3), ylim=c(0, 0.5), col="red", main =
  "HISTOGRAM WITH FITTED NORMAL CURVE", freq=F)
```

Finally, we create the fitted normal curve using the lines() command, along with dnorm().

```
lines(x, dnorm(x), lwd=2)
```

The output we get is as follows:

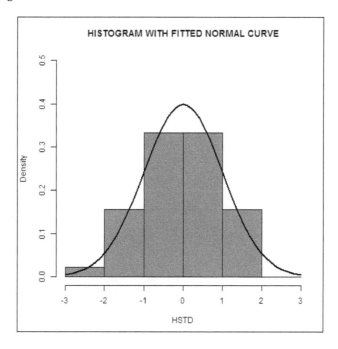

The histogram for height agrees nicely with the standard normal curve.

Creating boxplots

You can draw boxplots for individual variables or grouped variables. The syntax for boxplots is `boxplot(y~group, data=)`, where the argument `data=` refers to the data object. We use the syntax `y~group` to create a separate boxplot for each level of group. We use the argument `horizontal=TRUE` to reverse the axis.

The Modified Box Plot is the default in R. The Modified Box Plot highlights outliers while the Standard Box Plot does not. Let's start with a simple boxplot without specifying any groups. Again we use the medical dataset and create a boxplot for change in weight before and after treatment (that is, the difference between `WEIGHT_2` and `WEIGHT_1`). Ensure that the dataset is read into R and attached, as described earlier.

```
changewt <- WEIGHT_1 - WEIGHT_2
```

```
boxplot(changewt)
```

We now have a simple boxplot (as shown in the following graph) that gives the median and upper and lower quartiles of the data, and also indicates outliers:

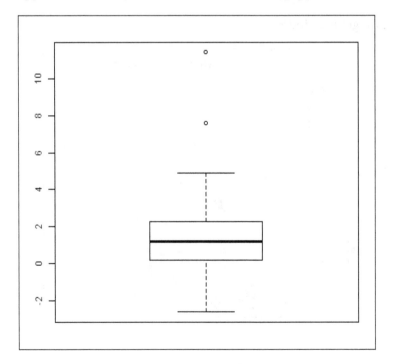

The top edge of the box gives the upper quartile (the value pertaining to the top quarter of the data). The lower edge of the box gives the lower quartile (the value pertaining to the bottom quarter of the data), and the heavy line gives the median. We have two outliers.

Note that the `boxplot()` command includes a `range` argument. The `range` argument determines how far the plot whiskers extend out from the box. If `range` is positive, the whiskers extend to the point(s) that is (are) no more than range times the interquartile range from the box. The argument `range = 0` ensures that the whiskers extend to the extreme points. In the previous graph, we have identified two outliers.

Now we will consider a grouped boxplot. Again we use the medical dataset and create a boxplot for change in weight for each treatment, using a nice ivory color from the Hexadecimal Color Chart. We use the formula `changewt ~ TREATMENT`:

```
boxplot(changewt ~ TREATMENT, data=T, main=toupper("WEIGHT CHANGE
    (kg)"), font.main=3, cex.main=1.2, xlab="Treatment ", ylab="Weight
        Change (kg)", font.lab=3, col="#FFFFCC")
```

We get the following boxplot for each level of the variable TREATMENT:

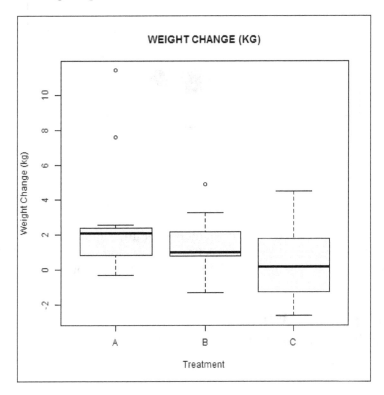

Now, we will create a notched boxplot of change in weight for each level of treatment (with different colors for each box). We use the argument `notch = T`. This time, we include the argument `range = 0` in order to ensure that the whiskers extend to the extreme points. Copy and paste the following syntax into R:

```
boxplot(changewt ~ TREATMENT, data=T, main=toupper("WEIGHT CHANGE
  (kg)"), font.main=3, cex.main=1.2, col=c("red","blue", "yellow"),
    xlab="Treatment", ylab="Change in Weight (Kg)", font.lab=3,
      notch=TRUE, range = 0)
```

The output is as follows:

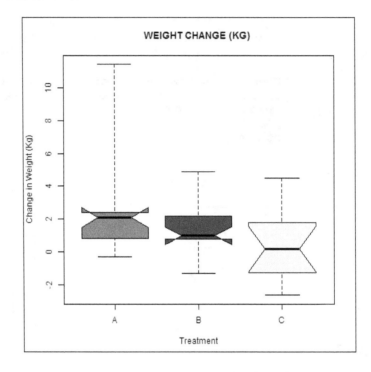

If the notches overlap, then there is no evidence for any significant difference in the medians across the groups. Here the notches overlap, and we conclude that there is no difference in median change in weight across the three treatments.

Creating pie charts

Let's create a simple pie chart from a vector of data:

```
J <- c(1, 8, 3, 9, 2, 5, 10)
```

```
pie(J)
```

The output is as follows:

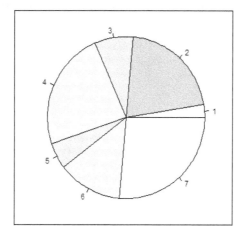

That was very easy. Now let's create a pie chart with a heading, using nice colors, and define our own labels using R's topo.colours palette. We control the number of colors using length(J). Why? Because length() counts the number of distinct elements in a vector and we need to count the colors.

We have seven measurements, one for each day of the week. Enter the following syntax, which includes the labels we wish to include in the pie chart:

```
pie(J, main="Daily Values", col=topo.colors(length(J)),

labels=c("Monday","Tuesday","Wednesday","Thursday","Friday","Saturday
  ","Sunday"))
```

Here is our pie chart with labels:

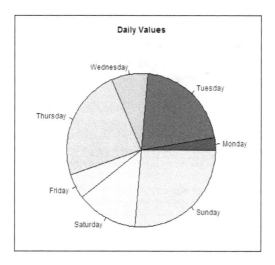

Let's create a pie chart of the numbers of patients receiving each treatment. First, we will create a table of counts of patients receiving each treatment:

```
table(TREATMENT)
```

The output is as follows:

```
TREATMENT
 A  B  C
16 17 12
```

Now, we apply the `pie()` command on this table of counts:

```
pie(table(TREATMENT))
```

Here is our pie chart:

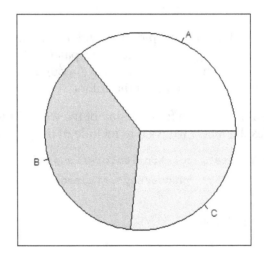

Now, we will create a more complex example, using percentages and a legend. We continue to use the data object J. We set up nice colors, again from the Hexadecimal Color Chart. Use the following syntax:

```
cols <- c("#FFFF33","#FF9999","#99CC99","#FF99FF",
  "#CCCCCC","#33FF00","#3366FF")
```

First, we calculate the percentage for each day. We round our percentage to one decimal place using the `round()` command. The syntax is as follows:

```
percentlabels <- round(100*J/sum(J), 1)
```

Now, we append a `%` sign to each percentage value using `paste()` as follows:

```
pielabels <- paste(percentlabels, "%", sep="")
pie(J, main="Daily Values", col=cols, labels=pielabels, cex=0.8)
```

Let's create a legend to the left using the following command:

```
legend("topleft", c("Monday","Tuesday","Wednesday",
  "Thursday","Friday","Saturday","Sunday"), cex=0.8, fill=cols)
```

Here is our pie chart:

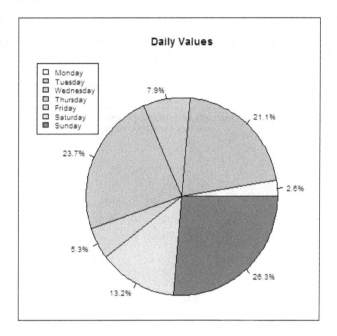

As another example, let's create a pie chart from the medical dataset and include numbers of patients receiving each treatment. We use the same table of counts as before.

```
table <- table(TREATMENT)
```

```
table
```

The output is as follows:

```
TREATMENT
 A  B  C
16 17 12
```

Now, we will create labels for each treatment, each consisting of the treatment level and the numbers of patients:

```
labs <- paste(names(table), " (",table,")", sep="")
```

```
labs
```

The result is as follows:

```
[1] ""A (16)"" ""B (17)"" ""C (12)""
```

Finally, we create the pie chart, along with labels, using the following syntax:

```
pie(table, labels = labs, col = c("#339999", "#006666", "#0099CC"),
  main="PIE CHART OF NUMBERS OF PATIENTS \nRECEIVING EACH TREATMENT")
```

Here is our pie chart with the numbers of patients for each treatment:

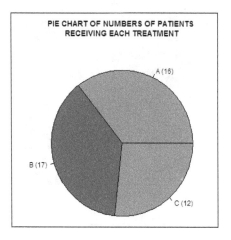

Note the use of \n just before the word RECEIVING. This syntax instructed R to write any following text on a new line.

Creating dotcharts

Again, let's use the medical dataset and create a dotchart of the heights of female patients. Dotcharts record a single measurement for each element in a dataset. Let's create the subset first. We will use the subset() command to select only female patients:

```
TF <- subset(T, GENDER =="F")
```

```
head(TF)
```

The output is as follows:

```
  PATIENT GENDER ETH TREATMENT AGE WEIGHT_1 WEIGHT_2 HEIGHT SMOKE EXERCISE RECOVER
1    Mary     F    1        A    Y     79.2     76.6    169    Y     TRUE       1
2    Jim      M    2        B    Y     87.5     84.8    178    Y     TRUE       0
3    Bob      M    2        A    M     65.1     64.6    162    N    FALSE       1
4    Dave     M    1        B    M     58.8     59.3    161    Y    FALSE       0
5   Simon     M    1        C    M     72.0     70.1    175    N    FALSE       1
6    Ben      M    3        A    Y     95.9     94.5    188    N    FALSE       1
```

Now, we will use the `dotchart()` command, include title and axis labels, modify the font sizes of the axis labels, and specify the row labels of the chart:

```
dotchart(TF$HEIGHT[1:6],labels=TF$PATIENT,cex=1.4, pch = 16,
  main="Female Patient Heights in Centimetres",xlab=toupper("Height
  (cm)"), xlim = c(130, 200), cex.lab = 0.7)
```

Our dotchart is as follows:

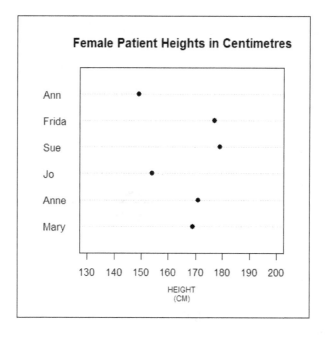

Notice that we specified the heights and patient names using the TF object and the dollar sign. This is because we had already attached the object T, and R has stored the variables HEIGHT and PATIENT for that object rather than for the new object TF. Specifying the object name avoids confusion between the two datasets.

Next, we consider a more complex dataset in which the data is arranged in columns, but where we want a dotchart of the entire dataset. We use the measurements dataset again and create another dotchart. This time, we take the transpose of the dataset using the transpose function t() as follows:

```
dotchart(t(measurements))
```

The dotchart obtained is as follows:

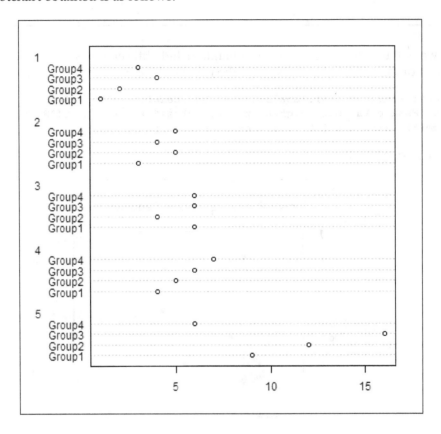

Note that R's dotchart() command accepts variables to be arranged in rows rather than in columns. That's why we took the transpose of the original data. Of course, you can embellish this dotchart using the usual approaches. We will use three symbol types and four colors as shown in the following syntax:

```
dotchart(t(measurements), xlim = c(0,20), pch = c(15:18), col =
    c("red", "blue", "darkgreen", "brown"), main = "Measurements for
      Four Groups", font.main = 2, xlab = "Measurements", cex.lab =
        1.2)
```

Now, the dotchart looks like this:

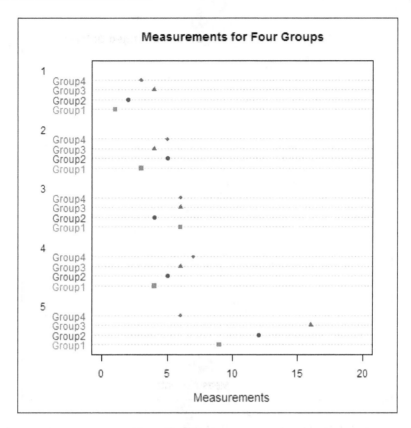

Now, we will create a slightly different dotchart with the same data, but using the `as.matrix()` command:

```
dotchart(as.matrix(measurements), xlim = c(0,20), pch = c(15:18), col
    = c("red", "blue", "darkgreen", "brown"), main = "Measurements for
        Four Groups arranged Differently", font.main = 2, xlab =
            "Measurements", cex.lab = 1.2)
```

Our dotchart now looks like this:

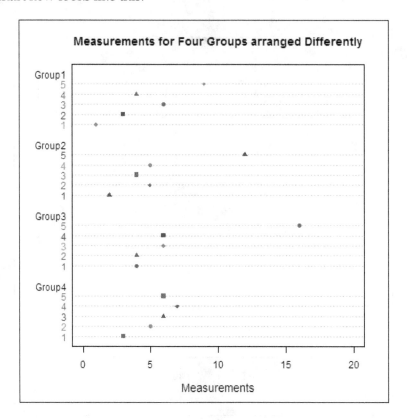

Let's put the two dotcharts together so that you can see the difference. We use `par()` and `mfrow = c(1,2)` to place them side-by-side. Copy and paste all of the following syntax together:

```
par(mfrow=c(1,2))
```

```
dotchart(t(measurements), xlim = c(0,20), pch = c(15:18), col = c("red",
"blue", "darkgreen", "brown"), main = "Scores for Four Groups", font.main
= 2, xlab = "Scores", cex.lab = 1.2)
```

```
dotchart(as.matrix(measurements), xlim = c(0,20), pch = c(15:18), col
  = c("red", "blue", "darkgreen", "brown"), main = "Scores for Four
    Groups arranged Differently", font.main = 2, xlab = "Scores",
      cex.lab = 1.2)
```

The dotchart obtained look like this:

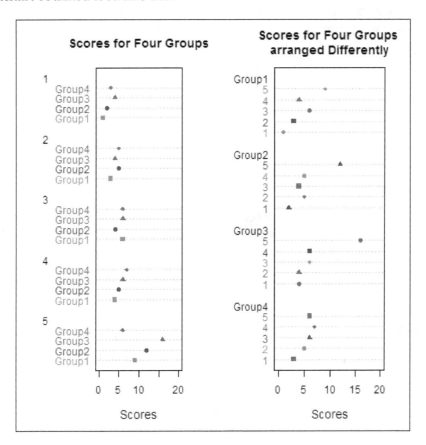

Can you see the difference? The first approach groups the data according to the measurements, while the second groups the data by the four groups.

Now, we will create a dotchart where the groups have different colors. We will create a dotchart of weight change by treatment. Let's remind ourselves of the levels of TREATMENT. We use the levels() command to do so:

```
levels(TREATMENT)
```

The output is as follows:

```
[1]  ""A""  ""B""  ""C""
```

Of course, we have three different treatments. Now, we wish to graph the change in body mass for each patient, sorted in order of change, but grouped by treatment. First, we recalculate weight change for each patient, bind this new variable into the array, and sort in ascending order of weight change. Use the following syntax to do so:

```
changewt <- WEIGHT_1 - WEIGHT_2
```

Next, we bind this variable to the array T. To do so, we use the cbind() function. We call the new version TCH:

```
    TCH <- cbind(T, changewt)
```

Enter TCH on the R command line to see that the new variable has indeed been included in the array.

Now, we sort the entire array in ascending order of the variable changewt. In general, if A is an array, you can sort A in ascending order by one of the variables (variable1) as follows:

```
A <- A[order(variable1), ]
```

To sort in descending order, use the following syntax:

```
A <- A[order(-variable1), ]
```

Let's apply this approach to the array TCH and sort in descending order of changewt:

```
TCH <- TCH[order(TCH$changewt),]
```

Enter TCH on the R command line to see that the array has been sorted in ascending order of weight change. Now, we will create a factor from the variable TREATMENT:

```
TCH$TREATMENT <- factor(TREATMENT)
```

```
TCH$TREATMENT
```

The output is as follows:

```
[1] A B A B C A A C B B A C A B A A B C A B B A C C A B B B C A A B A
A B C C B B A C B C C B
Levels: A B C
```

Let's give a different color to each level of TREATMENT to create our dotchart. We do this by subsetting with square brackets and reading in the desired colors to a new variable TCH$colour:

```
TCH$colour[TCH$TREATMENT == "A"]  <- "darkgreen"

TCH$colour[TCH$TREATMENT == "B"]  <- "red"

TCH$colour[TCH$TREATMENT == "C"]  <- "blue"
```

Now we create the dotchart as follows:

```
dotchart(TCH$changewt, labels=TCH$PATIENT, cex=.8, pch = 16, groups =
   TCH$TREATMENT,main="DOTCHART OF WEIGHT CHANGE BY TREATMENT",
     xlab="Weight Change (Kg)", cex.lab = 0.8, gcolor="black",
       color=TCH$colour)
```

The resulting graph is as follows:

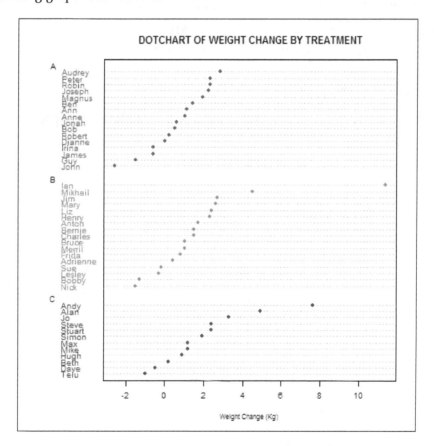

The dotchart has grouped the patients into an easy-to-understand chart, grouped by treatment.

R's color palettes

R's color palettes include the following: `Rainbow, heat.colors, terrain.colors, topo.colors,` and `cm.colors`.

You have already seen some of these palettes. For information on palettes in R, insert a question mark in front of the palette name, for example, `?terrain.colors`.

Using smoothers on your graph

Often it is useful to see a smooth version of your dataset that highlights trends or variations in the data that are not evident by examining the data directly. **LOWESS (locally weighted scatterplot smoothing)** is often used for this purpose. Here is an example of smoothing using LOWESS. We plot `HEIGHT` against `WEIGHT_2` and add a LOWESS smoother using the `lines()` and `lowess()` commands:

```
plot(WEIGHT_2, HEIGHT, main="LOWESS SMOOTHING EXAMPLE",
xlab="WEIGHT (kg) ", ylab="HEIGHT (cm)", pch=19)

lines(lowess(WEIGHT_2, HEIGHT), lwd=2, col="red")
```

Let's see the data with a smooth curve, as shown in the following graph:

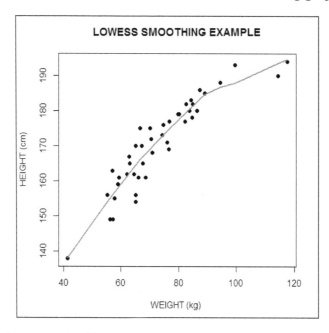

The smoother suggests some curvature to the data, which in this case was already evident in the raw data. In other cases, any trends or curvature might not be so apparent from the raw data, so a smoother might be very helpful.

Creating scatterplot matrices

Scatterplot matrices of bivariate data are helpful to identify relationships between variables in a dataset. We can create scatterplot matrices using pairs() and the tilde sign, along with plus signs that instruct R to include the desired variables:

```
pairs(~WEIGHT_1 + WEIGHT_2 + HEIGHT, data=T,
main="Scatterplot Matrix of Medical Data")
```

This syntax gives the following matrix:

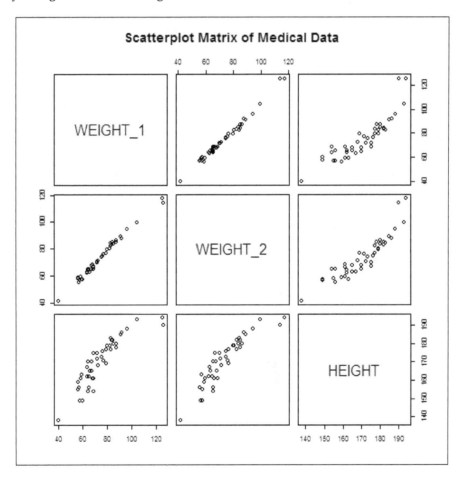

If we want a smooth curve (LOWESS) in each bivariate plot, we include the argument `panel=panel.smooth`:

```
pairs(~WEIGHT_1 + WEIGHT_2 + HEIGHT, data=T,
main="Scatterplot Matrix of Medical Data", panel = panel.smooth)
```

The matrix obtained is as follows:

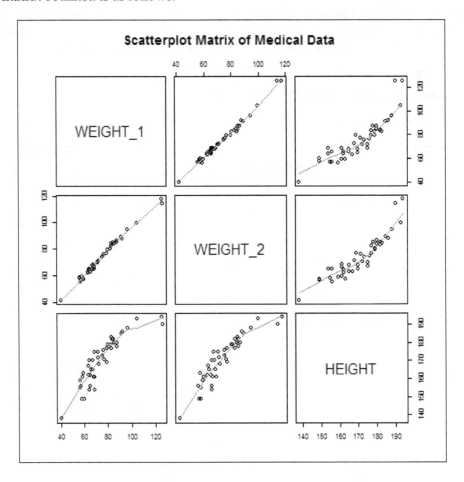

We see a strong linear relationship between WEIGHT_1 and WEIGHT_2, and curved relationships between those variables and HEIGHT.

Writing functions to create graphs

Why not create functions to draw graphs? Here's a function for histograms of vectors of data with standard titles and labels. It allows you to add numbers to the title and axis labels and choose the color. We use the `function()` command to set up a function that provides the attributes of our choice (for example, labels and title colors). Enter the following function on the R command line:

```
nicehist <- function(x, k, col) {
hist(x, main = paste("HISTOGRAM_", k, sep = ""),
xlab = paste("VALUES_", k, sep = ""),
ylab = paste("COUNTS_", k, sep = ""), col = col) }
f <- c(3,2,5,4,3,2,7,6,5,7,8,6,4,5,6)
```

Let's include 3 in the title and create a red histogram. Enter the following syntax:

```
nicehist(f, 3, "red")
```

The histogram obtained is as follows:

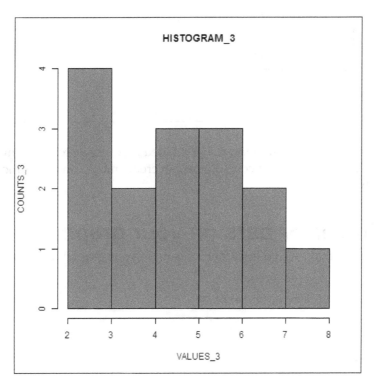

Let's include 99 in the title and create a light purple histogram.

```
nicehist(f, 99, "#FFCCFF")
```

The histogram now looks like this:

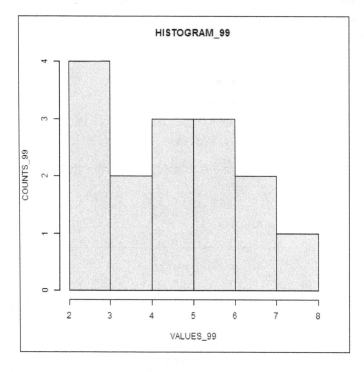

You can see that creating a function is a good idea if you have to create many similar plots and need to save time. Of course, you can create more complex function to create other types of graph.

Including error bars on your graph

Here is a function that I wrote to plot error bars on your graphs. Copy and paste it into R.

```
ploterrors <- function(w, z, err) {
zmin        <- z - err
zmax        <- z + err
HATWIDTH    <- 0.012
```

```
HAT   <-  HATWIDTH *( max(w) - min(w) )


for( k in 1:length(z) ) {


lines( c(w[k], w[k] ), c( z[k], zmin[k] ) , lwd = 0.8 )
lines( c(w[k], w[k] ), c( z[k], zmax[k] ) , lwd = 0.8 )


lines( c(w[k] - HAT, w[k] + HAT ), c( zmin[k], zmin[k] ), lwd = 0.8 )
lines( c(w[k] - HAT, w[k] + HAT ), c( zmax[k], zmax[k] ), lwd = 0.8 )
} }
```

Note that you can change the width parameter of the hat from my preferred value of 0.012 to some other number that gives you your preferred width. You can also vary the line width by changing lwd from 0.8 to your chosen value. Now, we will set up some data and a set of errors, and then we will plot:

```
X <- c(1,2,3,4,5,6,7,8)
Y <- c(1,2,3.4,5.6,7.8,10.3, 15.7, 18.3)
ERROR <- c(0.5, 1.2, 0.23, 2.21, 1.43, 1.28 , 2.18, 1.41)
plot(X, Y, xlab = "X VALUES", ylab = "Y VALUES", pch = 16)
lines(X, Y)
```

Now, we include the error bars using the function by including the horizontal and vertical axis variables and including the vector of errors as follows:

```
ploterrors(X, Y, ERROR)
```

We get the following graph that includes the data and error bars:

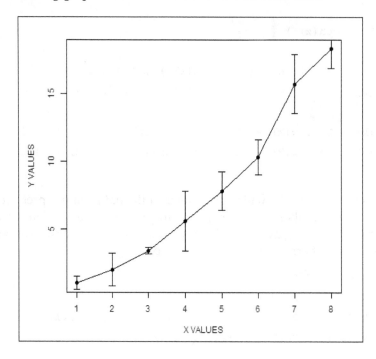

Summary

In this chapter, you learned some more of the basic syntax and techniques of producing graphs in R. We discussed more on regression lines and residuals — creating complex multiple axes, superposing graphs, labeling points on your graph, creating grid lines, shading and coloring graphs using the polygon() command, and so on. I hope this chapter provided a range of useful techniques in addition to those that you learned in the previous chapter.

The next chapter will continue from where we left off in this chapter. In the next chapter, we will learn how to create graphs using qplot, a very powerful graphics command that is available through the ggplot package.

3

Mastering the qplot Function

This chapter provides a step-by-step introduction to creating graphs using qplot (a graphics tool within the ggplot2 package), and gives examples of functioning qplot code that can be adapted for many applications. The topics covered in this chapter are as follows:

- Loading the ggplot2 package in order to use qplot
- Using basic qplot graphics techniques and syntax
- Creating scatterplots and line graphs
- Mapping symbol size, type, and color to categorical data
- Including regressions and confidence intervals in your graphs
- Creating bar charts, histograms, boxplots, pie charts, and dotcharts
- Creating time series graphs with dates

It is not possible to give a complete account of qplot in this book. However, by the end of this chapter, you should be able to use qplot to create a wide range of graphs for research and analysis.

About qplot

The qplot (quick plot) system is a subset of the ggplot2 (grammar of graphics) package, which you can use to create nice graphs easily. To use qplot, first install ggplot2. On the R command line, enter the following command:

```
install.packages("ggplot2")
```

Then load ggplot2 using this command:

```
library(ggplot2)
```

The qplot syntax

Let's assume that your data is loaded into R and now you wish to create a graph using the `qplot()` command. The generic `qplot` syntax is as follows:

```
qplot(x = X1, y = X2, data = X3, color = X4, shape = X5, size = X6,
  geom = X7, main = "Title")
```

Here, X represents the variables you wish to graph and the attributes you choose for your graph. You now have either univariate (one variable) or bivariate data (two variables), and you must provide instructions through the `geom` argument in order to create your graph. Now, let's explore some of the arguments in the `qplot` syntax:

- `data`: This argument refers to the dataset.
- `color`: This argument maps the color scheme onto a factor or numeric variable. Note that `qplot` selects default colors for each level of the variable. However, you can use special syntax to set your own colors.
- `shape`: This argument maps symbol shapes on to factor variables, and `qplot` uses different shapes for different levels of the factor variable. You can use special syntax to set your own shapes.
- `geom`: This argument allows you to select the type of graph, including: `"bar"`, `"histogram"`, `"line"`, and `"point"`.
- `main`: This argument allows you to provide a title.

In `ggplot2` (and therefore in `qplot`), color, size, and shape are known as aesthetic attributes. In `qplot`, you can set the aesthetics you like using the `I()` operator. For example, if you want symbols or lines in red, use `color = I("red")`. If you want to control the size of the symbols, use `size = I(N)`, where a value of N greater than 1 increases the size of the symbols. For example, `size = I(5)` produces very big symbols. On the other hand, you may wish to map color, size, and shape to levels of a factor variable. Shortly, you will see how this is done.

Producing scatterplots using qplot

Let's start with a simple example where we use the medical dataset that we saw in *Chapter 2, Advanced Functions in Base Graphics*. Again we cut and paste from the code file for this chapter. We invoke the `ggplot2` library, set up a simple scatterplot using red symbols, and save it as a PNG file. The syntax for invoking the library is as follows:

```
library(ggplot2)
```

Now let's plot `HEIGHT` against `WEIGHT_1`, using `I()` for color and symbol size. We choose red and a symbol size three times the `qplot` default size. Enter this syntax on the R command line:

```
qplot(HEIGHT, WEIGHT_1, data = T, xlab = "HEIGHT (cm)", ylab =
  "WEIGHT BEFORE TREATMENT (kg)" , color = I("red"), size = I(3))
```

After running the preceding command, you will get the following graph:

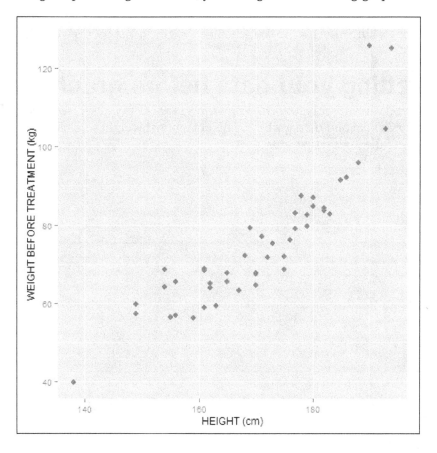

We get a scatterplot by default (that is, without specifying any `geom` argument). We see a plotting background that is gray in color and includes a grid. This is the default plotting background for `qplot`. Now let's save the graph as a PNG file with filename `fig_1.png`. You probably want to save your graph in a particular directory. To do so, you must ensure that this directory becomes your R "working directory".

You can set your R working directory by navigating to **File | Change Dir** and selecting the directory you wish to use. Now, enter these commands on the R command line:

```
png(filename = "fig_1.png")
qplot(HEIGHT, WEIGHT_1, data = T, xlab = "HEIGHT (cm)", ylab =
  "WEIGHT BEFORE TREATMENT (kg)" , color = I("red"), size = I(3))
dev.off()
```

Check your working directory to see whether the graph has been saved there.

Subsetting your data before graphing

Of course, you can subset before creating your graph. Let's subset T to include only females over 165 cm and then graph the height against weight. We use the subset() command and the logical operator &.

```
TF <- subset(T, GENDER ==  "F"  &  HEIGHT > 165)
TF
```

The dataset you get is as follows:

	PATIENT	GENDER	ETH	TREATMENT	AGE	WEIGHT_1	WEIGHT_2	HEIGHT	SMOKE	EXERCISE	RECOVER
1	Mary	F	1	A	Y	79.2	76.6	169	Y	TRUE	1
9	Anne	F	3	B	Y	77.1	76.1	171	Y	TRUE	0
15	Sue	F	1	A	M	79.6	79.8	179	N	TRUE	1
17	Frida	F	1	B	M	83.1	82.3	177	N	FALSE	0
21	Mike	F	2	B	E	72.2	71.0	168	Y	TRUE	1
28	Merril	F	2	B	M	75.3	74.3	173	N	FALSE	0
29	Beth	F	1	C	E	67.6	67.4	170	N	TRUE	1
42	Irina	F	1	B	M	64.7	65.3	170	N	FALSE	0

Now let's create a graph of height against weight for this smaller dataset using the following syntax:

```
qplot(HEIGHT, WEIGHT_1, data = TF,  geom = c("point"), xlab =
  "HEIGHT", ylab = "WEIGHT")
```

Here is our graph:

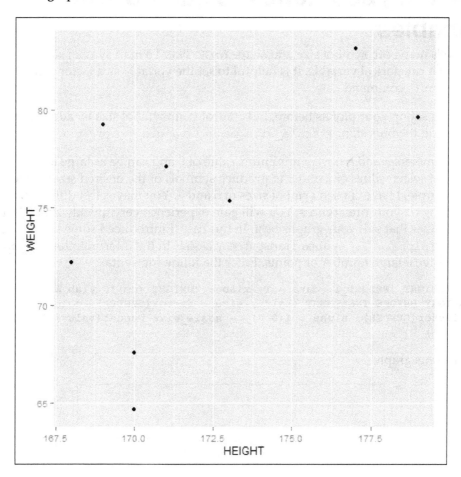

As an exercise, you can create another scatterplot that is similar to the preceding scatterplot, again using the argument geom = "point". Enter the following syntax and create the graph for yourself:

```
qplot(HEIGHT, WEIGHT_1, data = T, geom = "point", xlab = "HEIGHT
  (cm)", ylab = "WEIGHT BEFORE TREATMENT (kg)" , color = I("red"),
    size = I(3))
```

Mapping aesthetics to categorical variables

Now let's map both symbol size and shape to GENDER. To map symbol size to levels of a categorical variable, it is helpful to set the variable as a factor using the factor() command.

Then you set up your plot as before, but control your symbol size by adding a new layer using the plus sign: + scale_size_manual(values = c(a, b)).

The parameters a and b have a minimum value of 0 and can be as large as you like. You must select values of a and b to produce symbols of the desired size. In the next example, I have chosen symbol sizes of 5 and 7. You may select different sizes, depending on your preferences. You will gain experience very quickly and select the symbol sizes that suit your graphs best. In this case, I introduced some transparency using the alpha = I() syntax. Transparency assists in the interpretation of graphs that involve a large number of points. Enter the following syntax:

```
qplot(HEIGHT, WEIGHT_1, data = T, xlab = "HEIGHT (cm)", ylab =
  "WEIGHT BEFORE TREATMENT (kg)" , size = factor(GENDER), color =
    factor(GENDER), alpha = I(0.7)) + scale_size_manual(values = c(5,
      7))
```

You get this graph:

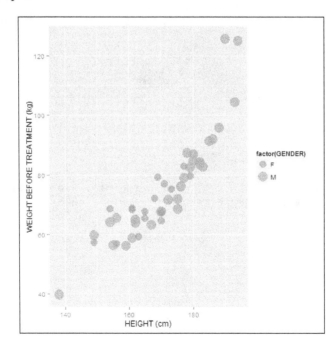

Our graph looks good, but the legend title includes the word **factor**. We shall see how to fix this problem in a later example. For now, enter the following syntax:

```
qplot(HEIGHT, WEIGHT_1, data = T, xlab = "HEIGHT (cm)", ylab =
  "WEIGHT BEFORE TREATMENT (kg)" , size = factor(GENDER), color =
    factor(GENDER), alpha = I(0.7))
```

We mapped the size and color to one variable (in this case GENDER), but we can map each of these aesthetics to a different factor variable. Let's map the symbol size to one variable (GENDER) and color to another variable (EXERCISE) using the arguments size and color.

```
qplot(HEIGHT, WEIGHT_1, data = T, geom = c("point"), xlab = "HEIGHT
  (cm)", ylab = "WEIGHT BEFORE TREATMENT (kg)" , size =
    factor(GENDER), color = factor(EXERCISE)) +
      scale_size_manual(values = c(5, 7))
```

Now you get a graph like this one:

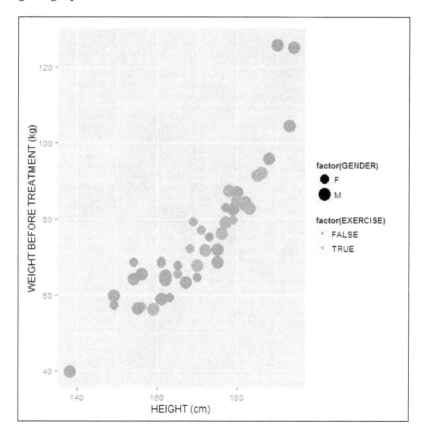

Controlling colors on your graph

Now let's map the symbol size to GENDER and the symbol color to EXERCISE. To control your symbol colors, use the layer scale_color_manual() and select your desired colors. We choose red and blue and symbol sizes 3 and 7, as shown in the following syntax:

```
qplot(HEIGHT, WEIGHT_1, data = T, geom = c("point"), xlab = "HEIGHT
  (cm)", ylab = "WEIGHT BEFORE TREATMENT (kg)" , size =
    factor(GENDER), color = factor(EXERCISE)) +
      scale_size_manual(values = c(3, 7)) +
        scale_color_manual(values = c("red","blue"))
```

Here is our graph with red and blue points:

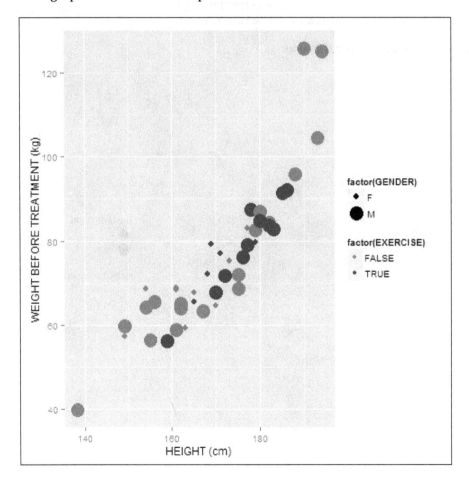

Now you know how to choose you own color scheme for your qplot graphs. Mapping color to categorical data can give us additional insight into the relationships that exist between variables.

Now let's see how to control the legend title (the title that sits directly above the legend). For this example, we control the legend title through the name argument within the two functions scale_size_manual() and scale_color_manual(). Enter the following syntax:

```
qplot(HEIGHT, WEIGHT_1, data = T, geom = c("point"), xlab = "HEIGHT
  (cm)", ylab = "WEIGHT BEFORE TREATMENT (kg)" , size =
    factor(GENDER), color = factor(EXERCISE)) +
      scale_size_manual(values = c(3, 7), name="Gender") +
        scale_color_manual(values = c("red","blue"),name="Exercise")
```

Our graph now includes a better legend title:

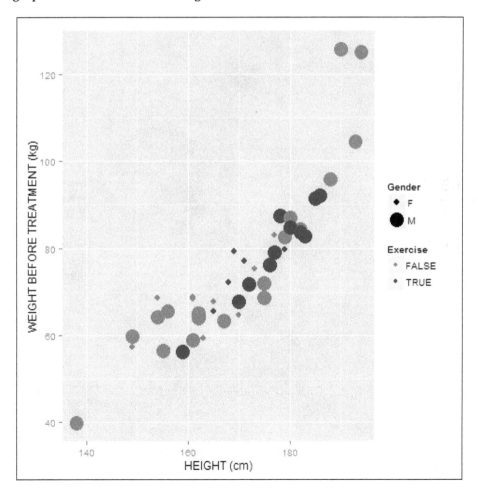

By including the arguments `name="Gender"` and `name="Exercise"` in the relevant function, we were able to control the legend title and include the variable names without the word `factor`. In the examples of the remainder of this chapter, we will omit this technique in order to simplify the syntax presented with each example.

Now let's create a similar graph, but including transparency using `alpha = I()`. We choose a value of `0.3` to illustrate the effect of transparency quite clearly. Enter the following syntax:

```
qplot(HEIGHT, WEIGHT_1, data = T, alpha = I(0.3), geom = c("point"),
  xlab = "HEIGHT (cm)", ylab = "WEIGHT BEFORE TREATMENT (kg)" , size
    = factor(GENDER), color = factor(EXERCISE)) +
      scale_size_manual(values = c(3, 7), name="Gender") +
        scale_color_manual(values = c("red","blue"),name="Exercise")
```

The output is as follows:

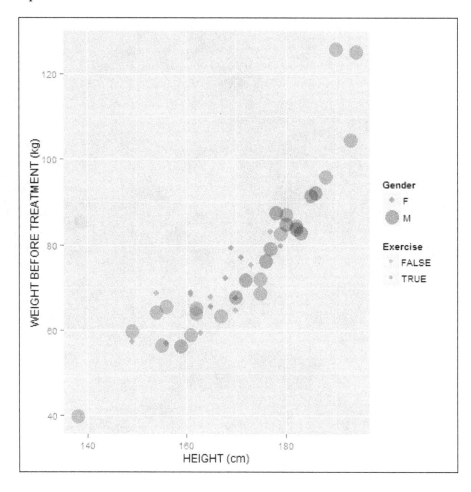

We can control transparency using either decimals or fractions. Rather than `I(0.7)`, we could use `I(7/10)`.

Setting up graphs as objects

We can set up the initial graphing syntax as an object. In the next example, we call this object `Y`. We can use any object name, as long as it starts with an alphabetic character. We map the symbol `color` to `ETH`, a categorical variable of three levels. Then, we impose our own colors by adding the new colors as a layer to the object `Y`:

```
Y <- qplot(HEIGHT, WEIGHT_1, data = T, main = "HEIGHT vs. WEIGHT",
  xlab = "HEIGHT (cm)", ylab = "WEIGHT BEFORE TREATMENT (kg)" , geom
    = "point" , color = factor(ETH), size = 2, alpha = I(0.7))
```

```
Y + scale_color_manual(values = c("darkgreen","red", "yellow"))
```

The output is as follows:

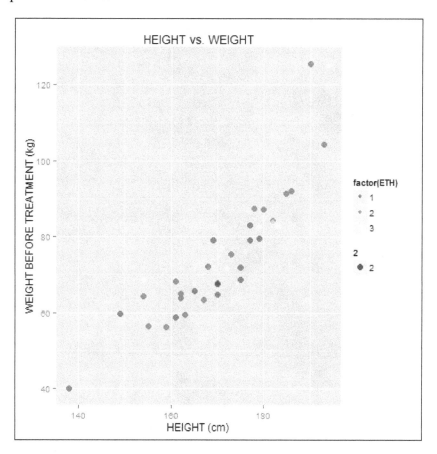

Setting up graphs as objects can be very useful. Using your initial object, you can try out different color schemes, symbol types, and other attributes until you get the appearance you want.

Creating facet plots

If you have a large dataset that includes a categorical variable, you can use the `facets` command to produce multiple graphs: one for each level of the categorical variable. In the following example, we will create a graph for each level of ETH (1, 2, and 3) using `facets = ETH ~ .`. Note the tilde sign followed by the period. Enter this syntax:

```
qplot(HEIGHT, WEIGHT_1, data = T,  geom = "point",  main = "HEIGHT
  VS. WEIGHT BY ETHNICITY", xlab = "WEIGHT BEFORE TREATMENT (Kg)",
    ylab = "HEIGHT (cm)", facets = ETH ~ .)
```

Our facet plot is as follows:

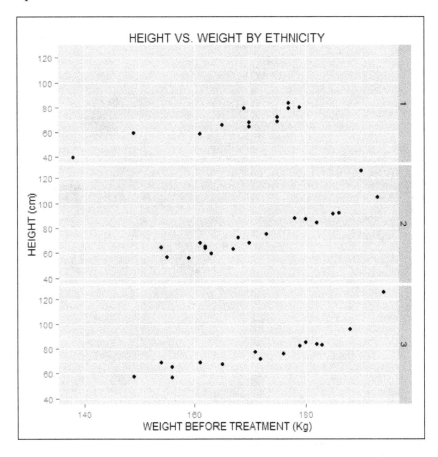

Indeed, we have three scatterplots arranged vertically: one for each level of
ETHNICITY. We can also create facet plots across the levels of two factor variables. In
the following code, we will create a scatterplot of HEIGHT against WEIGHT_1 for each
combination of SMOKE and EXERCISE in each facet, where the two levels of gender
are represented by shape and color. Here is the required command:

```
qplot(HEIGHT, WEIGHT_1, data=T, shape=factor(GENDER),
  color=factor(GENDER),facets=SMOKE ~ EXERCISE, size=I(3),
    xlab="HEIGHT", ylab="WEIGHT BEFORE TREATMENT", main = "HEIGHT vs.
      WEIGHT")
```

You will get the following output:

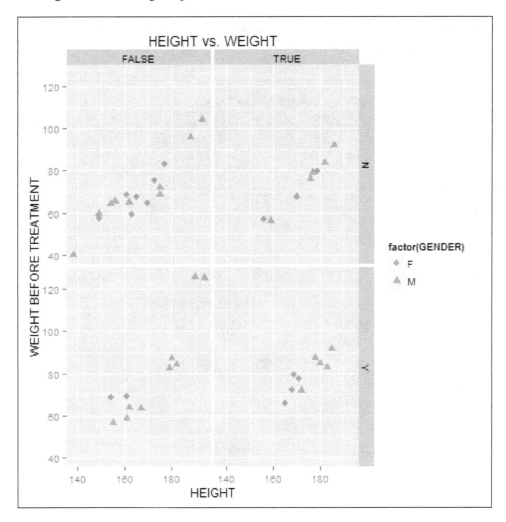

Since SMOKE and EXERCISE are both categorical variables of two levels, we ended up with four graphs—one for each combination of the two levels. Note the syntax `facets=SMOKE ~ EXERCISE`.

Creating line graphs using qplot

You can create line graphs using `geom = "line"`. The methods for mapping size and color that you have just seen still apply when you include both lines and symbols on the same graph. In the following code, we will map line color to the three levels of the variable `ETH` to produce three curves on the same graph:

```
qplot(HEIGHT, WEIGHT_1, data = T, geom = "line", color =
   factor(ETH), main = "Height vs. Weight before Treatment")
```

Here is the resulting graph:

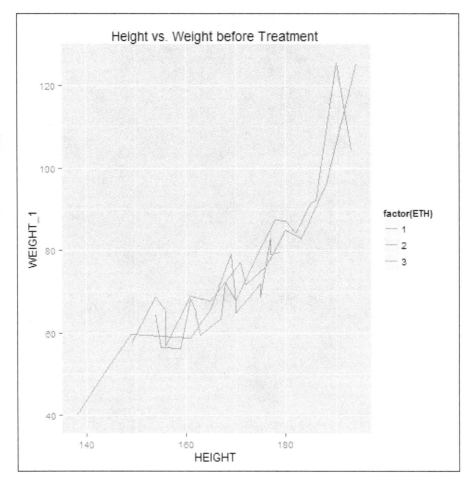

Use the `linetype` = argument to vary your line types. Try the following examples:

```
qplot(HEIGHT, WEIGHT_1, data=T, geom="line",
  group=TREATMENT)
qplot(HEIGHT, WEIGHT_1, data=T, geom="line",
  linetype=as.factor(TREATMENT))
qplot(HEIGHT, WEIGHT_1, data=T,  geom="line", linetype=
  as.factor(TREATMENT), color= as.factor(TREATMENT))
```

Let's take a look at the last of the graphs obtained using the above syntax:

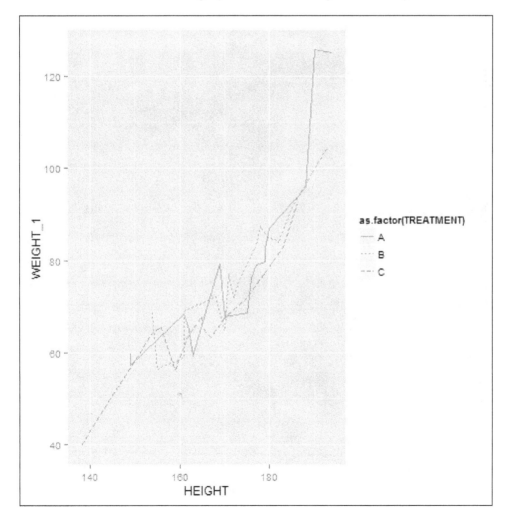

We see a different line type and color for each level of treatment. Now let's create a graph similar to the previous one, but include both points and lines using `geom = c("point", "line")`.

```
qplot(HEIGHT, WEIGHT_1, data = T, geom = c("line", "point"), color =
  factor(ETH), main = "Height vs. Weight before Treatment")
```

Here is the resulting graph:

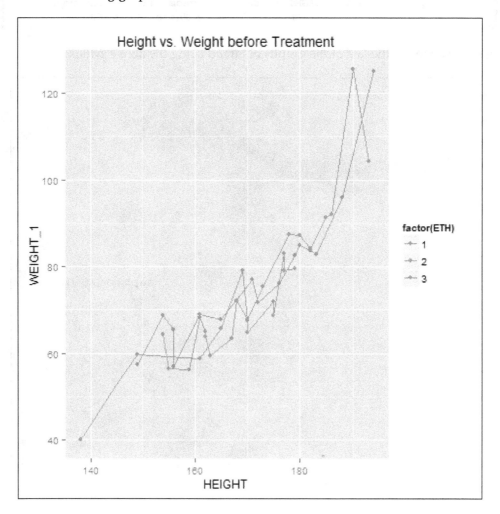

The graph now includes both points and lines.

Creating multiple curves simultaneously

Now let's learn how to create several curves in one graph, provided that the data is arranged correctly. Read the `Children` dataset from the code file of this chapter. It gives the heights and ages of four children. We want to produce a graph of **Height** against **Age** for each child, including both points and lines. Enter the following command:

```
attach(cheight)
```

Let's see the first eight rows of this dataset:

```
head(cheight, 8)
```

We get the following output:

```
  Child  Age Height
1  John   13    165
2  John   14    172
3  John   15    174
4  John   16    177
5  John   17    179
6  John   18    181
7  Mary   13    145
8  Mary   14    153
```

Note that the data is arranged in columns so that several measurements for each child appear in a single column. This format is ideal for creating multiple curves simultaneously. Before we start, let's remind ourselves of the names of each child. Since `Child` is a categorical variable, we can see each name using the `levels()` command:

```
levels(Child)
```

Their names are:

```
[1] "Anne" "Joe" "John" "Mary"
```

Let's plot all curves together in the same graph, mapping `color` to `Child` with the following command:

```
qplot(Age, Height, data = cheight, geom = c("line","point"),
color = Child, main = "Growth Patterns of Four Children")
```

We get the following graph:

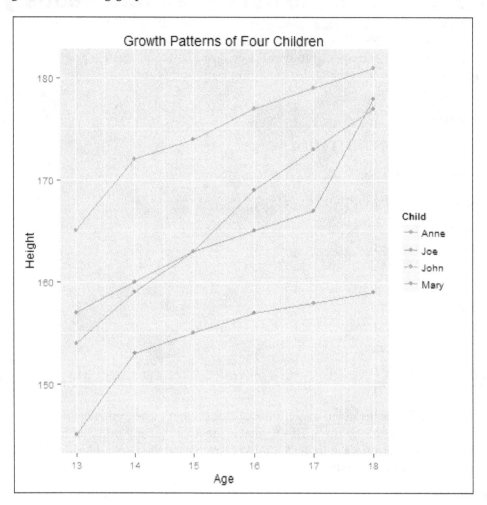

We now have a colored curve and colored points for each child.

Including smoothed curves

Let's create a scatterplot relating height and weight before treatment, along with both points and a smooth curve using `geom = c("point","smooth")`. In qplot, the default smoother is LOWESS, and the gray band represents a standard error confidence interval. LOWESS fits models to local subsets of the variables to produce a smoothed version of the data.

You can read further about LOWESS in various texts and online sources. For this example, we set up the graph as an object (Y) and plot it by entering the object name on the command line:

```
Y <- qplot(HEIGHT, WEIGHT_1, data = T, xlab = "HEIGHT (cm)", ylab =
  "WEIGHT BEFORE TREATMENT (kg)", geom = c( "point","smooth"))
```

```
Y
```

Our graph now looks like this:

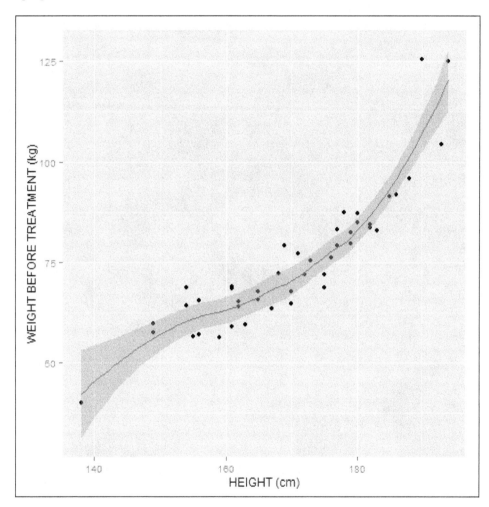

We have the smoothed curve and the confidence interval. Let's graph the same data, but map color to ethnicity. We add transparency in order to make the curves easy to interpret. The syntax is as follows:

```
Y <- qplot(HEIGHT, WEIGHT_1, data = T, xlab = "HEIGHT (cm)", ylab =
"WEIGHT BEFORE TREATMENT (kg)" , geom = c("point","smooth"), color =
factor(ETH), alpha = I(0.2))


Y
```

Here is the resulting graph:

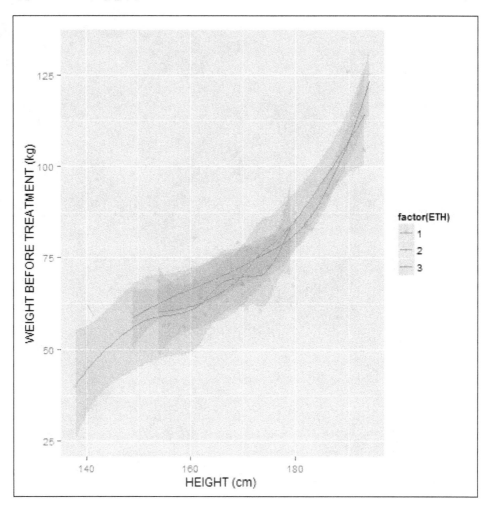

As before, to select your own colors for the smoothed curves, add the `scale_color_manual()` layer, for example:

```
Y + scale_color_manual(values = c("darkgreen", "red", "yellow"))
```

The graph now looks like this:

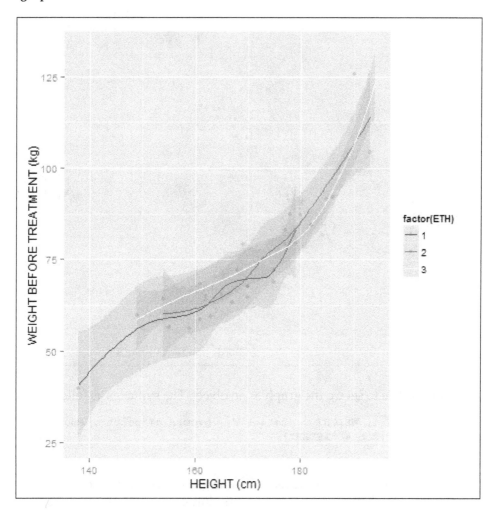

As we saw in the previous example, qplot often provides several ways of achieving the same graph. Here we set up the graph first, and then specify geom later using the plus sign. Here, we plot weight before treatment against weight after treatment using the following syntax:

```
qplot(WEIGHT_1, WEIGHT_2, data = T, xlab = "BEFORE", ylab = "AFTER")
  + geom_smooth()
```

The graph looks like this:

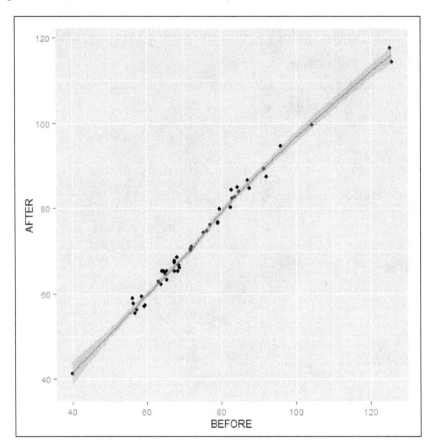

Another approach is to set up the graph as an object. The syntax is as follows:

```
p <- qplot(WEIGHT_1, WEIGHT_2, data = T,  geom = c("point","smooth"),
xlab = "BEFORE", ylab = "AFTER")

p
```

Notice that these approaches produced the same graph. Now let's use a linear regression model to obtain the smooth curve (in this case, a straight line). To fit a linear regression model, use the argument `method = "lm"`, as follows:

```
qplot(WEIGHT_1, WEIGHT_2, data = T,  geom = c("point","smooth"),
  xlab = "BEFORE", ylab = "AFTER", method = "lm")
```

Here is the graph:

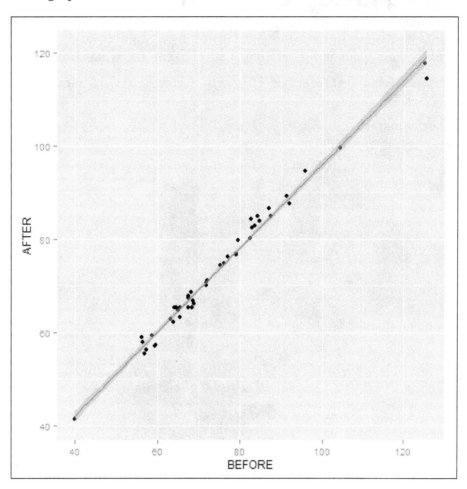

The regression shows a highly linear relationship between the two measurements, so that the standard error confidence band is very narrow.

In fact, qplot provides various smoothers, of which LOWESS is the default. Other options include OLS regression and generalized additive models. You can control the width of the smoother using the span argument. For example, span = 0.2 gives a wider band and span = 1 (the maximum value of span) gives a narrower band. You can modify the smoothed curve by varying the span value between 0 (not smooth) and 1 (smooth).

Creating histograms with qplot

Now, let's learn how to create a histogram using geom = "histogram" and control the bin width using the argument binwidth. In this example, we will create a histogram of the heights of the patients and select a bin width of 10 cm. The syntax is as follows:

```
qplot(HEIGHT, geom = "histogram",  ylab = "COUNT", xlab = "HEIGHT",
  binwidth = 10)
```

Here is our histogram:

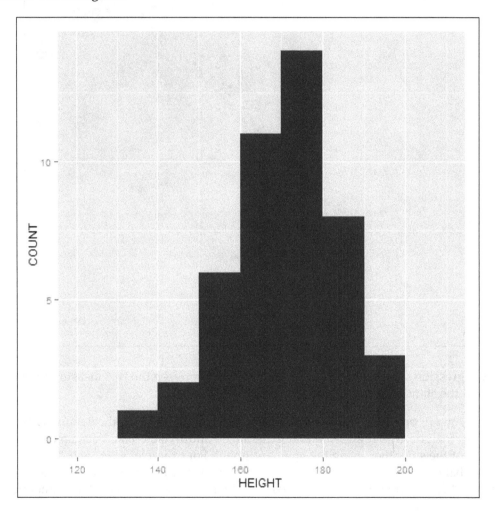

Our histogram has a rather chunky appearance, and we may wish to change the color and other attributes of the default histogram. By the way, note what happens if we use the syntax `color = I("blue")`:

```
qplot(HEIGHT, geom = "histogram",  ylab = "COUNT", xlab = "HEIGHT",
  binwidth = 10, color = I("blue"), fill = I("wheat"))
```

Now the histogram looks like this:

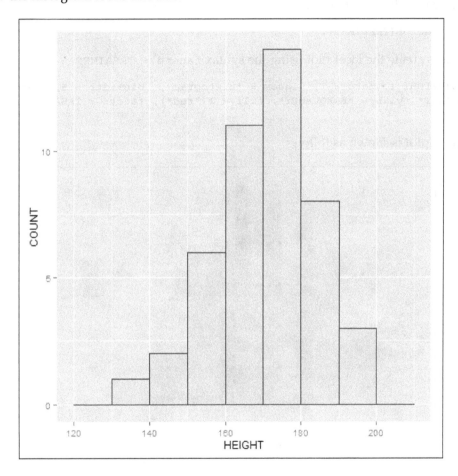

We get blue outlines for the bars and the axes. Remember that, for histograms, the `color` argument controls the color of the histogram outlines, while the argument `fill` controls the color of the bars.

Creating facet plots for histograms

As with scatterplots, we can create facet plots for histograms. This technique is useful when we have one or more categorical variables and wish to obtain histograms for each level or combination of levels. Let's create a histogram facet plot of weight before treatment for each level of treatment. First, we turn TREATMENT into a factor. To create facet plots across the levels of a categorical variable, first turn the variable into a factor using the following syntax:

```
TRC <- factor(TREATMENT)
```

Now, let's create the facet plot using the syntax facets = TREATMENT ~ .

```
qplot(WEIGHT_1, data = T,   geom = "histogram",  binwidth = 5, xlab =
  "WEIGHT", ylab = "FREQUENCY", fill = I("red"), facets = TREATMENT ~
  .)
```

The facet plot is shown as follows:

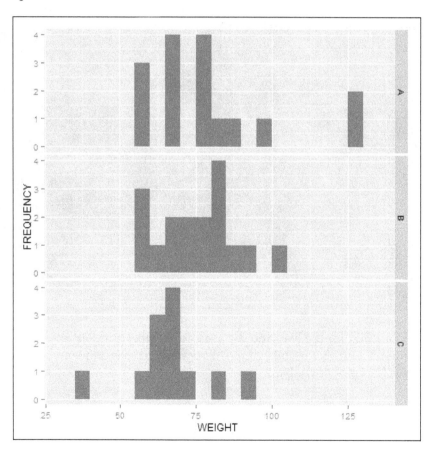

We now have a histogram for each level of TREATMENT. Facet plots provide additional detail about the variability of the critical variables.

Creating kernel density plots

Let's create a kernel density plot for patient height. The kernel density plot is essentially a smoothed version of a histogram. A full discussion of kernel density plots is beyond the scope of this book, but for many applications they provide a viable alternative to the histogram. We use a bin width of 5 cm, though we could try other bin widths. Enter the following syntax:

```
qplot( HEIGHT, data = T,   geom = "density",  binwidth = 5, xlab =
  "HEIGHT (cm)", ylab = "DENSITY")
```

The kernel density plot looks like this:

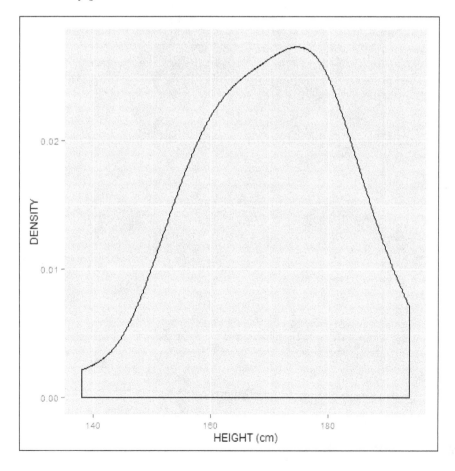

In a kernel density plot, the height of the curve gives an estimate of the probability density at the given value along the horizontal axis.

To shade underneath a density plot, you can use the `polygon()` command. In the following example, we will illustrate how this is done in base graphics. Here, we select a light green color and use the default smoothing (that is, we do not specify a bin width). Enter the following syntax:

```
plot(density(HEIGHT), xlab = "HEIGHT (cm)", ylab = "DENSITY", main =
  "HEIGHT DENSITY PLOT")
```

```
polygon(density(HEIGHT), col="#66FF99", border="darkgreen")
```

We get this graph:

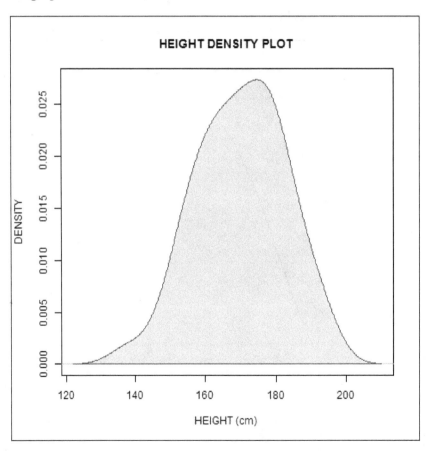

The `polygon()` command has shaded under the curve exactly as we wished.

Now let's see how shading is done in `qplot`. We create a kernel density plot for height, grouped by gender and mapped to our own choice of color. We add transparency in order to make the plot easy to interpret. The `fill` argument gives a second method of shading under a density plot. Enter the following syntax:

```
Y <- qplot(HEIGHT, data=T, geom="density", fill=factor(GENDER),
  alpha=I(0.5), main="Height by Gender", xlab="Height (cm)",
    ylab="Density ")
```

```
Y + scale_fill_manual(values = c("red", "yellow"))
```

Now the graph looks like this:

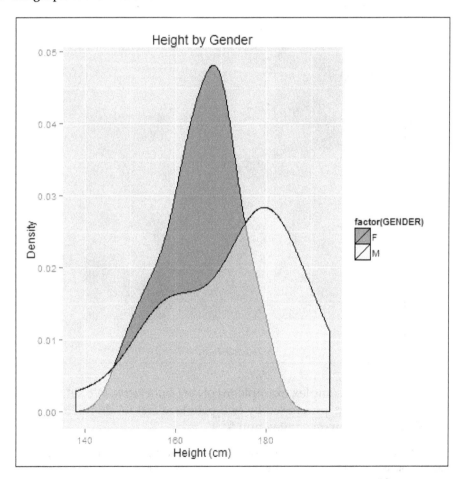

Note that the overlapping area of the two plots has its own color. In this case, the overlapping area is colored orange.

Creating bar charts

Now, let's use `qplot` to produce a frequency bar chart; in this case, for the categorical variable TREATMENT. The heights of the bars give the counts of patients receiving each treatment. We choose a nice hue of brown from the Hexadecimal Color Chart. To create a bar chart, we use `geom = "bar"`. Enter the following syntax:

```
qplot(TREATMENT, data = T, geom = "bar",  binwidth = 5, xlab =
  "HEIGHT (cm)", ylab = "FREQUENCY", fill = I("#CC6600"), color =
    I("blue"))
```

Here is our bar chart:

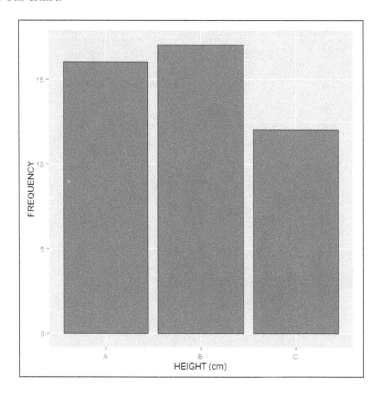

The following is a more complex example involving bar charts. We set up a new dataset relating to dinners purchased by two people at fast food outlets during one week. Enter the following syntax into R:

```
dinners = data.frame(person=c("Thomas", "Thomas", "Thomas", "James",
  "James"), meal = c("curry", "stew", "salad", "fish", "stir-fry"),
    price = c(15, 18, 12, 25, 13))


dinners
```

The output is as follows:

	person	meal	price
1	Thomas	curry	15
2	Thomas	stew	18
3	Thomas	salad	12
4	James	fish	25
5	James	stir-fry	13

Let's plot the number of dinners each person purchased that week. We choose a nice hue of purple from the Hexadecimal Color Chart. Enter the following syntax:

```
qplot(person, data = dinners, geom = "bar", ylab = "Meals", fill =
  I("#9999CC"))
```

Here is our bar chart of the number of dinners:

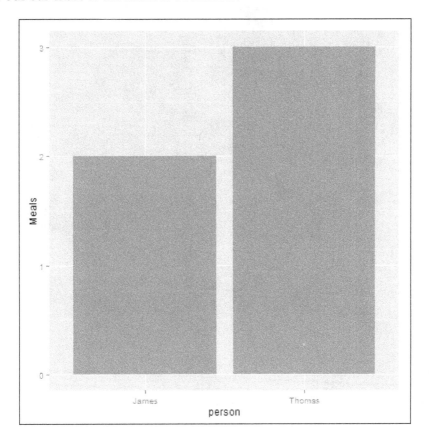

By default, the height of each bar gives a count of the number of dinners purchased by each person. However, if we want to graph the total cost of each person's dinners, we must provide a different weight; in this case, the price variable. The weight is simply the variable that we wish to evaluate and plot on our bar graph. We choose a nice hue of green. Enter the following syntax:

```
qplot(person, weight = price, data = dinners, fill = I("#009933"),
  geom = "bar", ylab = "Total Cost ($)")
```

The bar chart now looks like the following:

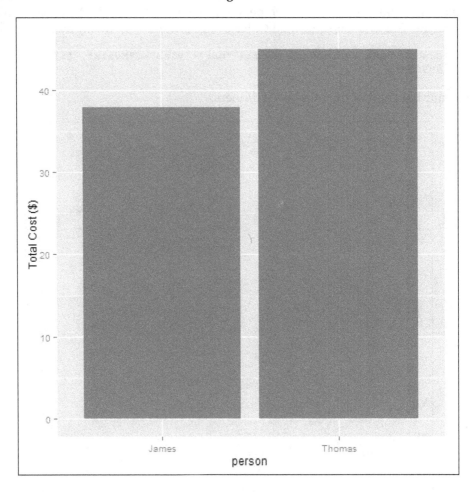

Now the height of each bar represents the total cost of each person's dinners.

Creating boxplots

In this section, we will learn how to create boxplots. Using the medical dataset, let's produce a simple boxplot of patient weight before treatment, grouped by the three levels of treatment. We use the syntax `geom = "boxplot"` and again we choose a nice color from the Hexadecimal Color Chart. Enter the following syntax:

```
qplot(TREATMENT, WEIGHT_2, data = T,   geom = "boxplot",   xlab = "
    TREATMENT", ylab = "WEIGHT (kg)", fill = I("#99CCFF"))
```

Here is the boxplot:

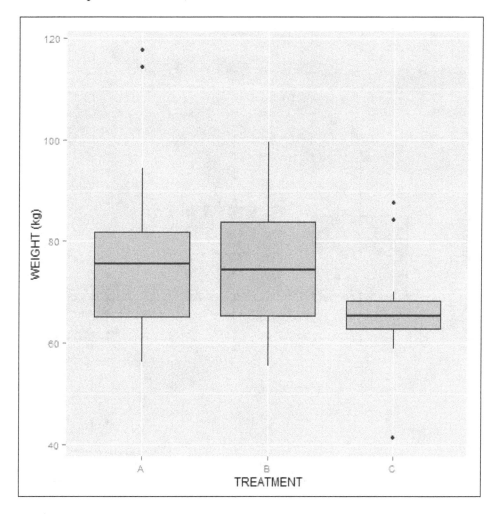

If we do not wish to create a grouped boxplot and want a boxplot of all of the data taken together, we simply omit the categorical variable from the qplot() command. Anyway, within any boxplot, we can include the data as points—positioned according to the levels of the factor variable. Simply include "point" within geom as follows:

```
qplot(TREATMENT, WEIGHT_2, data = T, geom = c("boxplot","point"),
  xlab = "TREATMENT", ylab = "WEIGHT (kg)", fill =
    I("#669900"))
```

The boxplot, along with the raw data, looks like this:

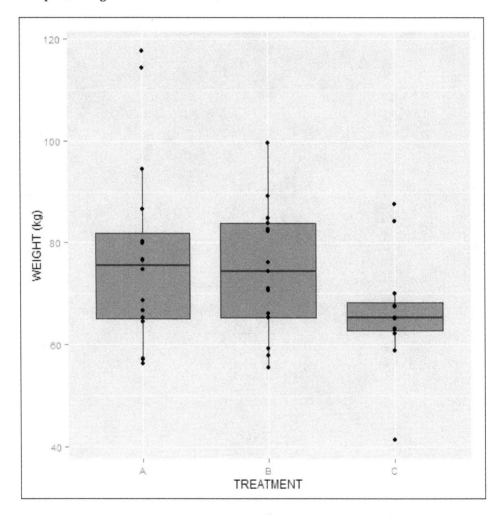

Including the data gives us additional insight into the variation of weight across the three levels. Now, let's create a box for each level of ethnicity using `as.factor()`, or simply `factor(cyl)`. Again, we use the Hexadecimal Color Chart to give a different color to each box. To do this, we use the `c()` operator to include three colors within `fill = I()`. Enter the following syntax into R:

```
qplot(as.factor(ETH), WEIGHT_2, data = T,   geom = "boxplot", xlab =
   "ETHNICITY", ylab = "WEIGHT (kg)", fill = I(c("#66CC99", "#9999CC",
      "#CC6666")))
```

Now the boxplot looks like this:

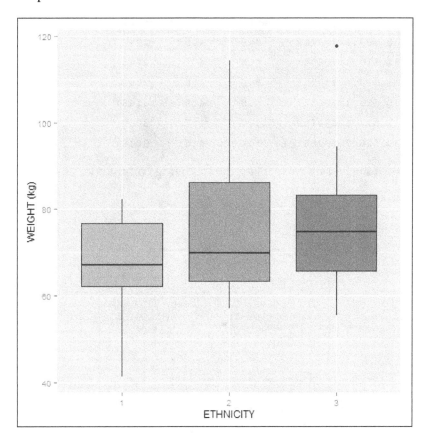

We have produced an attractive boxplot with different colors for each box. Remember that if the categorical variable is not initially a factor, then you can turn it into a factor using either `as.factor()` or `factor()`. Then, you can proceed to create your grouped boxplot.

Creating graphs with dates

Sometimes, you may wish to create a time series graph that involves dates along the horizontal axis. We can create such graphs using qplot. Let's try plotting a time series graph. We use the built-in economics dataset (see http://docs.ggplot2. org/current/economics.html) and plot the population against the date. Let's see the first six rows using head():

```
head(economics)
```

Here are the first six rows of the data:

```
        date     pce    pop   psavert  uempmed  unemploy
1 1967-06-30  507.8  198712    9.8      4.5      2944
2 1967-07-31  510.9  198911    9.8      4.7      2945
3 1967-08-31  516.7  199113    9.0      4.6      2958
4 1967-09-30  513.3  199311    9.8      4.9      3143
5 1967-10-31  518.5  199498    9.7      4.7      3066
6 1967-11-30  526.2  199657    9.4      4.8      3018
```

Now we look at the last six rows using the following command:

```
tail(economics)
```

The output is as follows:

```
           date  variable   value
11 2006-06-30        pop  299801
12 2006-07-31        pop  300065
13 2006-08-31        pop  300326
14 2006-09-30        pop  300592
15 2006-10-31        pop  300836
16 2006-11-30        pop  301070
17 2006-12-31        pop  301296
18 2007-01-31        pop  301481
19 2007-02-28        pop  301684
20 2007-03-31        pop  301913
41 2006-06-30   unemploy    7228
42 2006-07-31   unemploy    7116
43 2006-08-31   unemploy    6912
44 2006-09-30   unemploy    6715
45 2006-10-31   unemploy    6826
46 2006-11-30   unemploy    6849
47 2006-12-31   unemploy    7017
48 2007-01-31   unemploy    6865
49 2007-02-28   unemploy    6724
50 2007-03-31   unemploy    6801
```

We can see that the economics dataset runs from the year 1967 to 2007 and contains dates in a particular format (hyphens separate the year, month, and day). We wish to plot certain variables by date. However, before we plot, note that R likes dates in the format year-month-day. For example, let's extract the first date in the economics dataset:

```
economics$date[1]
```

The output is as follows:

```
[1] "1967-06-30"
```

You can use the `as.Date()` function to ensure that R understands a particular format. For example, November 3, 2011 may be expressed as 03/11/2011. However, R does not yet understand this format. Let's read this format into R.

```
date1 <- "03/11/2011"
date1
```

The output obtained is as follows:

```
[1] "03/11/2011"
```

We cannot use this format directly, but we can express the date in the format in which R likes dates. Enter the following syntax:

```
date1B <- as.Date(date1, "%d/%m/%Y")
date1B
```

Now the output is:

```
[1] "2011-11-03"
```

Note the percentage signs. The lowercase m stands for the month, the lowercase d stands for the day of the month, and finally the uppercase Y stands for the year. Other examples may involve the lowercase b (an abbreviation of the name of the month; for example, Mar) or the uppercase B, which refers to the full name of the month. You can convert other formats to the necessary format using `as.Date()` and percentage signs. For example, you can use the following syntax:

```
as.Date('12MAR89',format='%d%b%y')
```

```
 [1] "1989-03-12"
```

Now use the following syntax:

```
as.Date('August 11, 1987',format='%B %d, %Y')
```

```
 [1] "1987-08-11"
```

In these examples, you can see that we recast the given date to the preferred format for R by instructing R how to interpret each component of the given date.

Let's create our graph, placing date as the first argument inside the `qplot()` command. Enter the following syntax:

```
qplot(date, pop, data=economics, geom="line", col = I("red"), size =
    I(2))
```

You will get this graph:

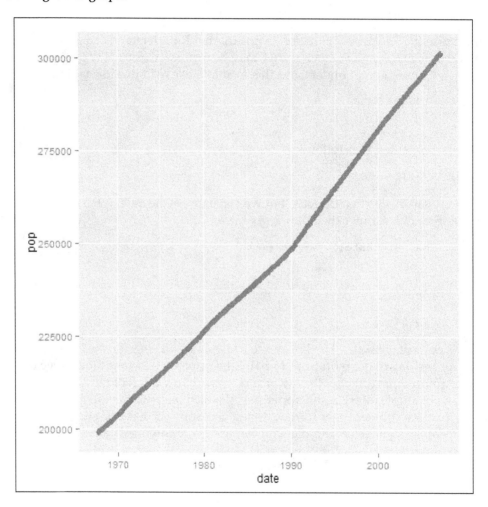

The graph has horizontal axis labels for every decade. For datasets spanning shorter periods of time, `qplot` may produce default axis labels for each year or even for each month.

Now, let's plot against a particular set of dates that are labeled appropriately. We will select only data pertaining to `2006-6-1` and after. We use the `subset()` command and the comparison operator `>` to select our set of dates:

```
econdata <- subset(economics, date > as.Date("2006-6-1"))
econdata
```

We get the following output:

	date	pce	pop	psavert	uempmed	unemploy
469	2006-06-30	9338.9	299801	-1.7	8.2	7228
470	2006-07-31	9352.7	300065	-1.5	8.4	7116
471	2006-08-31	9348.5	300326	-1.0	8.1	6912
472	2006-09-30	9376.0	300592	-0.8	8.0	6715
473	2006-10-31	9410.8	300836	-0.9	8.2	6826
474	2006-11-30	9478.5	301070	-1.1	7.3	6849
475	2006-12-31	9540.3	301296	-0.9	8.1	7017
476	2007-01-31	9610.6	301481	-1.0	8.1	6865
477	2007-02-28	9653.0	301684	-0.7	8.5	6724
478	2007-03-31	9705.0	301913	-1.3	8.7	6801

Now let's create our graph, a line graph in red and twice the default line width, using the following syntax:

```
qplot(date, pop, data=econdata, geom="line", col = I("red"), size =
  I(2))
```

Here is the output graph:

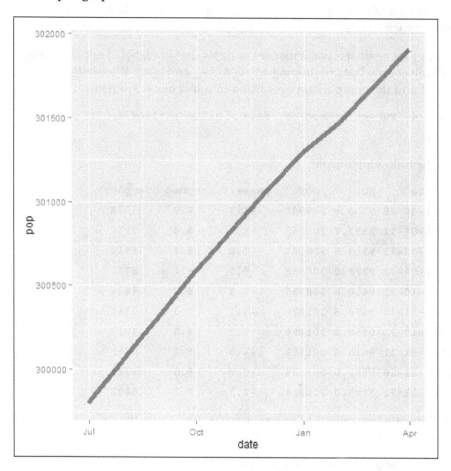

So far, we have plotted one variable (pop). However, the variables are configured in separate columns (one variable to each column), whereas qplot needs all of the variables we wish to plot in a single column. So, how do we plot two or more of the variables on the same graph? To create graphs of one or more variables in our dataset (pce, pop, psavert, and so on), we use the melt() function (provided within the reshape package) in order to configure the data into a format that qplot can use. The reshape package provides functions that enable you to recast data into formats that are suitable for qplot and ggplot. The melt() function creates a new column that stores the variables. To use the functions provided within reshape, first install the reshape package by entering install.packages("reshape") on the command line. Then, load the reshape library using the library() command:

```
library(reshape)
```

Now we use the `melt()` command:

```
dat <- melt(econdata, id = "date")
head(dat)
```

The output is as follows:

	date	variable	value
1	2006-06-30	pce	9338.9
2	2006-07-31	pce	9352.7
3	2006-08-31	pce	9348.5
4	2006-09-30	pce	9376.0
5	2006-10-31	pce	9410.8
6	2006-11-30	pce	9478.5

Note that all of the variables are now arranged column-wise and given the column name `variable`. It makes sense to plot both population and unemployment together, because they are related variables and because the other variables exist on completely different scales. Therefore, we subset for these two variables only. We use the logical operator for OR (the vertical line) to include data for `pop` and `unemploy` together:

```
datsub <- subset(dat, variable == "pop" | variable == "unemploy")
```

```
datsub
```

You will get the following output:

	date	variable	value
11	2006-06-30	pop	299801
12	2006-07-31	pop	300065
13	2006-08-31	pop	300326
14	2006-09-30	pop	300592
15	2006-10-31	pop	300836
16	2006-11-30	pop	301070
17	2006-12-31	pop	301296
18	2007-01-31	pop	301481
19	2007-02-28	pop	301684
20	2007-03-31	pop	301913
41	2006-06-30	unemploy	7228
42	2006-07-31	unemploy	7116
43	2006-08-31	unemploy	6912

```
44  2006-09-30  unemploy      6715
45  2006-10-31  unemploy      6826
46  2006-11-30  unemploy      6849
47  2006-12-31  unemploy      7017
48  2007-01-31  unemploy      6865
49  2007-02-28  unemploy      6724
50  2007-03-31  unemploy      6801
```

Now we make the variables of this object visible to R by name using `attach()`:

```
attach(datsub)
```

Now let's use `qplot` to plot the two series, mapping a color to each variable:

```
qplot(date, value, data = datsub, type = "point", size = I(3), id =
    variable, color = variable)
```

Here is our graph:

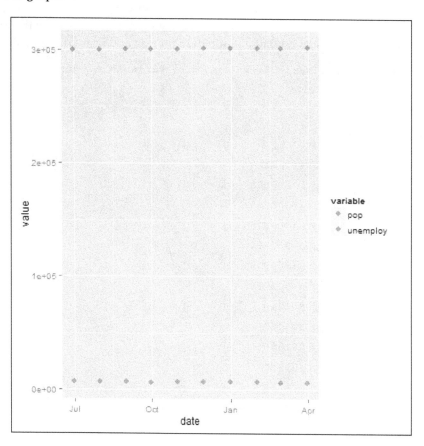

These two series are of different magnitudes, but at least we have included them on the same graph. Note that the date axis includes labels (giving the month) in quarters (that is, where the calendar year is divided into four quarters).

Navigate to `http://docs.ggplot2.org/current/`, and refer to `scale_x_date` for examples of plotting multiple times series on a single graph.

One last example will suffice to illustrate the formatting options available through `qplot`. We load the `scales` library in order to access various date formatting functions. The `scales` library enables us to choose the format we want for labels on our time series graphs. For example, we may wish to provide axis labels in the format month/day. We use `scale_x_date()` to do this job:

```
library(scales)
```

```
W <-  qplot(date, value, data = datsub, type = "point", size = I(3),
    id = variable, color = variable)
```

```
W + scale_x_date(labels = date_format("%m/%d"))
```

The graph looks like this:

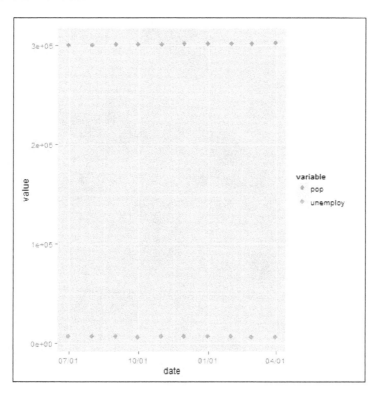

Our graph includes dates (quarterly) according to the required format: month/day.

Summary

In this chapter, you learned a variety of useful techniques to produce high-quality graphs using qplot. You also learned how to create scatterplots, line graphs, and many other types of graph. You also saw how useful qplot can be when you want to map symbol size, shape, and color (or linetype) to levels of a categorical variable. In a book of this scope, it is impossible to cover all of the possibilities available through qplot, but I hope you found that this chapter provided helpful approaches that you can use to create your own graphs. Many books and online sources on qplot are available for you to develop your qplot skills even further.

In the next chapter, you will learn how to create graphs using the ggplot function, an even more powerful graphics command.

4
Creating Graphs with ggplot

In the previous chapter, you learned a variety of useful techniques to produce high-quality graphs using qplot. In this chapter, you will learn how to create graphs using ggplot, an even more powerful graphics tool than qplot. In a book of this scope, it is impossible to cover all that ggplot has to offer. Thus, here we learn only the basic methods of ggplot. After reading this chapter, you should be able to create interesting graphics using ggplot. If you wish to read further about ggplot, links to other literature are given in this chapter. The topics covered in this chapter include the following:

- Setting up variables for plotting
- Adding color, symbol type, size, and shape as layers
- Controlling plotting backgrounds and margins
- Creating line graphs, histograms, bar chats, and boxplots
- Using attractive color schemes

By the end of this chapter, you should understand the basic principles behind the creation of graphics in ggplot, and will be able to create professional graphs with ggplot.

To assist you in mastering ggplot, I recommend the website http://docs.ggplot2.org/current/.
This website provides links that assist you in a wide range of ggplot techniques.

Getting started with ggplot

You may find that qplot is sufficient to create most of the graphics you want. However, you may need even more options than are provided within qplot, and ggplot may provide those options. Mastering ggplot is somewhat more difficult than qplot, but ggplot does provide more options to control plotting backgrounds, axes and axis labels, legends, grids, and color schemes.

In ggplot, we set up an initial graphing object and then add attributes in steps (which we call layers). Let's start by creating a scatterplot of patient height versus weight before treatment using the medical dataset, which you can copy and paste from the code file for this chapter (available in the code bundle of this book). First note the aes() function (**aes** is short for the word **aesthetics**) in which we identify the variables that we wish to include in our graph and in which we set up mappings for color, size, and shape. Also, note the geom_point() function that creates points. Thus, we now set up HEIGHT and WEIGHT_1 as the variables we wish to graph using aes() and then we add the layer geom_point() to create a scatterplot. Later, we can add symbol types (colors, shapes, and sizes, and so on) as new layers. Enter the following syntax, which creates a graphics object:

```
library(ggplot2)

P <- ggplot(T, aes(x = HEIGHT, y = WEIGHT_1)) + geom_point()
P
```

Here is the scatterplot of patients' height versus weight:

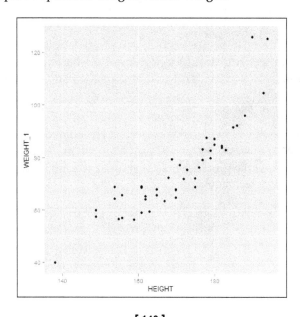

The two variables you wished to plot were included within the `aes()` function and the instruction to plot points (rather than a line) was provided though the `geom_point()` function. We can include axis labels that record the units of measurement using `xlab()` and `ylab()`. We can use this syntax:

```
P + xlab("HEIGHT (cm)") + ylab("WEIGHT_1 (Kg)")
```

However, we will use the `labs()` function instead and we now include a title using `labs(title...)`:

```
P + labs(x = "HEIGHT (cm)", y = "WEIGHT_1 (Kg)") + labs(title =
  "WEIGHT vs. HEIGHT_1")
```

Here is our scatterplot:

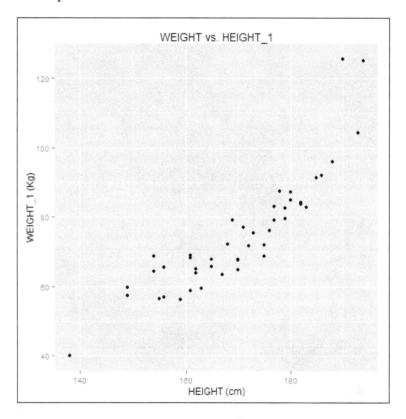

Again, the horizontal and vertical axis labels and the title were added as layers. Let's update the graphics object P so that from now on our graph has a title and axis labels that give the units of measurement. Enter the following syntax:

```
P <- P + labs(x = "HEIGHT (cm)", y = "WEIGHT_1 (Kg)") + labs(title =
  "WEIGHT vs. HEIGHT")
```

At this stage, we may wish to modify the title. Let's set the title to twice the default size and set its color to blue. To do so, we make use of `plot.title` within the `theme()` function, which allows you to modify theme settings. We also make use of the function `element_text()`, which allows you to modify color, size, font, and other attributes of your text. In the following syntax, we increase the font size using `size = rel()`:

```
P + theme(plot.title = element_text(size = rel(2), color = "blue"))
```

This syntax gives us the following scatterplot:

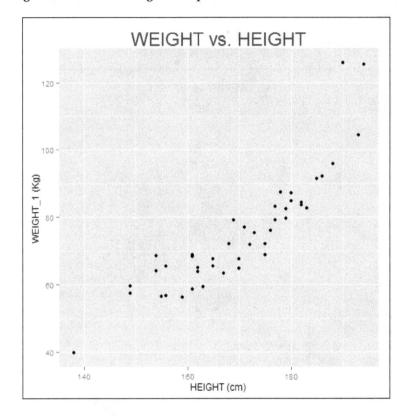

You can see that some complex syntax was required. However, now that you know the syntax, you can use it to modify titles in your own graphs. Further information on the themes available in `ggplot` is given in various texts and online sources. A very good resource is available at `http://docs.ggplot2.org/current/theme.html`.

In the *Producing scatterplots using qplot* section in *Chapter 3, Mastering the qplot Function*, we saw how to set aesthetics in `qplot`. In ggplot, the aesthetics are set within a function that also controls the graph type. For example, we have `geom_point()` for scatterplots, `geom_bar()` for bar graphs, and `geom_histogram()` for histograms. In the following syntax, we use points, and then set the symbol color to dark green and the symbol size to the value 5:

```
P + geom_point(color = "darkgreen", size = 5)
```

Here is the resulting scatterplot:

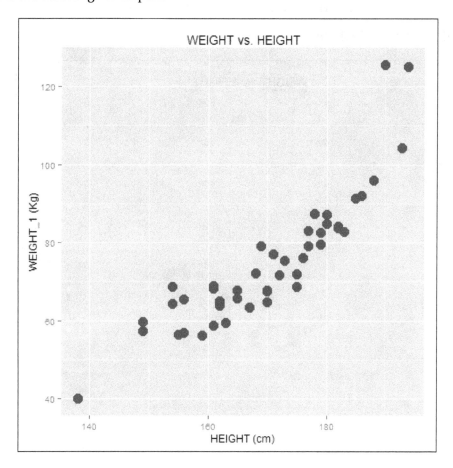

Mapping color, shape, and size to a variable

We saw how to map a color to a categorical variable using `qplot`. Now we map symbol color to the three levels of `ETH` using `ggplot`. In `ggplot`, we map color, size, and shape within `aes()`; also, as we did in `qplot`, we select our own color scheme using `scale_color_manual()`, as follows:

```
P + geom_point(aes(color = factor(ETH)), size=I(5)) +
  scale_color_manual(values = c("red", "yellow", "blue"))
```

Now the scatterplot looks like this:

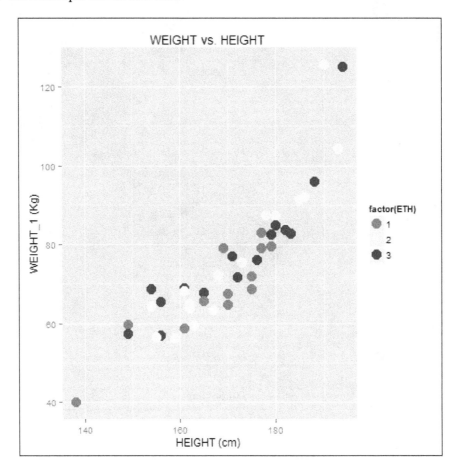

Each level of ETH now has a different color. In ggplot, we can also map symbol size and shape to factor levels, again using aes(). Try the following code yourself:

```
P + geom_point(aes(size = factor(ETH)))
```

You will get this scatterplot:

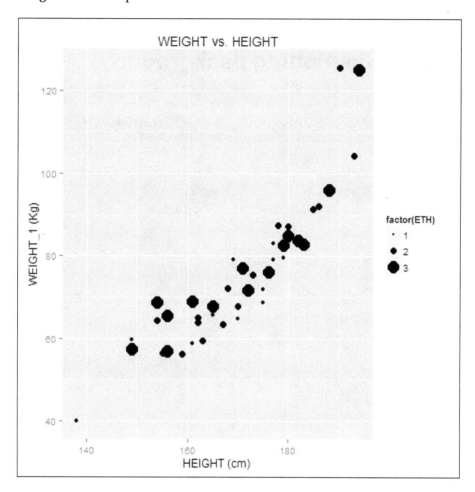

Another way of mapping symbol size is through scale_size_area(). Try the following code yourself:

```
P + geom_point(aes(size = WEIGHT_2)) + scale_size_area()
```

The `scale_size_area()` layer maps symbol area onto continuous variables by dividing the continuous variable into levels. Try the following syntax yourself. It uses another function called `scale_shape()`. In this example, we create a nice effect by including two sets of symbols:

```
P + geom_point(aes(shape = factor(TREATMENT)), size = 3) +
   scale_shape(solid = FALSE)
```

Modifying the plotting background

You can change the appearance of the plotting background using various themes. The default theme is `theme_grey()`, which gives a gray background with white grid lines. Let's create a white background using `theme_bw()`, which by default produces black grid lines:

```
P + theme_bw()
```

Here is the resulting scatterplot:

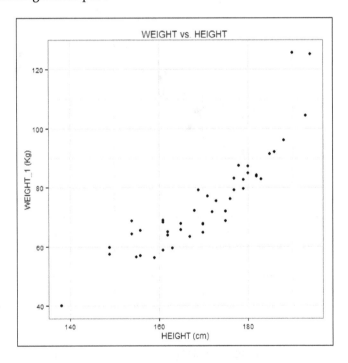

You can change both your panel and plot attributes using `theme()`. For example, if you want the ivory color for the background, you can get it using `theme(panel.background = element_rect(fill = "ivory"))`, as shown:

```
P + theme(panel.background = element_rect(fill = "ivory"))
```

This syntax gives us the following scatterplot:

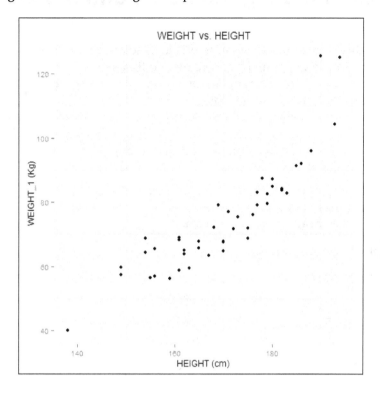

Again, you require some complex syntax, but you can use this syntax to provide any color you like for your plotting background. Of course, ggplot allows you to control almost every aspect of a graph. For example, you can perform the following actions:

- Color the plotting margin using plot.background.
- Modify gridlines using panel.grid.major and panel.grid.minor.
- Introduce transparency using the alpha argument within the geom function.
- Control the legend position using theme(legend.position...).
- Change your legend keys using theme(legend.key...). For example, you can change the legend labels, create a nice box around your legend, color the legend space, or write the legend title in italics.
- Modify tick marks and tick labels using theme(axis.text...).
- Create horizontal and vertical lines using geom_hline() and geom_vline().

The website given in the introduction to this chapter (http://docs.ggplot2.org/current/) provides links that assist you with all of the previous techniques and many others.

Controlling the legend name and legend labels

As we saw with `qplot`, mapping an aesthetic to a factor variable can change the legend name by introducing the word `factor`. To fix this problem, use the `name` argument in one or other of the many scale options. We can also modify the legend labels using `labels`. In the next example, we create our own legend name and assign particular ethnicities to the levels of `ETH`. At the same time, we encounter a very useful function, `scale_color_brewer()`. This function allows you to select from a wide range of color palettes (the default option is a range of blue hues). The syntax is as follows:

```
P + geom_point(aes(color = factor(ETH)), size= I(4)) +
  scale_color_brewer(name = "Ethnicity",
    labels=c("European","Asian","Other"))
```

The scatterplot looks as follows:

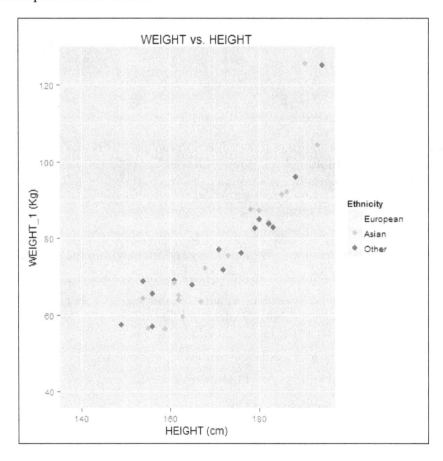

We have succeeded in naming our legend as we wished, and we have met a new function that allows you to choose attractive color schemes. Note that we used `scale_color_brewer()` only after mapping color to ETH within aes.

Modifying the x and y axes

Both `scale_x_continuous()` and `scale_y_continuous()` are very useful functions. They provide many options for modifying axes. For example, you can use these functions to control axis limits, reverse the axes, and introduce logarithmic or other axis scales. In addition, they provide yet another way of creating axis labels. Try the following syntax yourself:

```
P + scale_x_continuous("Centimetres") +
  scale_y_continuous("Kilograms")
```

However, these two functions can do a lot more. For example, let's use `scale_x_continuous` and `scale_y_continuous` to modify our axis limits.

```
P + scale_y_continuous(limits=c(60, 100)) +
  scale_x_continuous(limits=c(140, 180))
```

We get this graph:

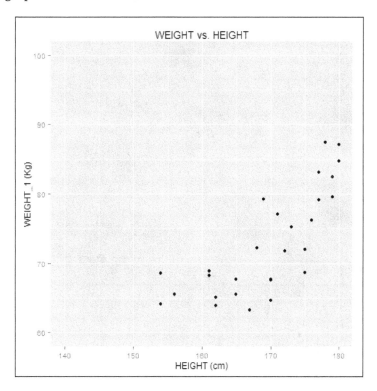

Within these two functions, you can select locations for tick marks using `breaks`. Try this syntax yourself:

```
P + scale_x_continuous(breaks=c(150, 160, 180)) +
  scale_y_continuous(breaks=c(70, 90, 120))
```

You can label the ticks as you wish using `labels`:

```
P + scale_x_continuous(breaks=c(150, 160, 180), labels=c("SMALL",
  "MEDIUM", "LARGE"))
```

Here is the resulting graph:

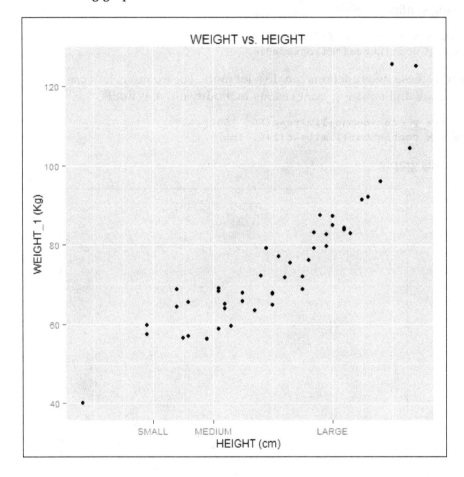

Creating attractive color schemes

You saw how to use `scale_color_brewer` to create various color schemes, starting with a range of blues (the default color scheme). While using this function, you must select the palette you wish to use. The `scale_color_brewer()` function uses syntax like this:

```
scale_color_brewer(..., type =  , palette = )
```

You can select either `seq` (sequential), `div` (diverging), or `qual` (qualitative). Within those options, you can then select a particular palette, where the available palettes control color schemes. Further information on `scale_color_brewer()` can be found at `http://docs.ggplot2.org/current/scale_brewer.html`.

Try all of the following lines of syntax yourself:

```
P + geom_point(aes(color = factor(ETH)), size=I(4)) +
  scale_color_brewer(type="div")


P + geom_point(aes(color = factor(ETH)), size=I(4)) +
  scale_color_brewer(palette="Greens")


P + geom_point(aes(color = factor(ETH)), size=I(4)) +
  scale_color_brewer(type="seq", palette=3)


P + geom_point(aes(color = factor(ETH)), size=I(4)) +
  scale_color_brewer(type="seq", palette=4)


P + geom_point(aes(color = factor(ETH)), size=I(4)) +
  scale_color_brewer(type="seq", palette=6)


P + geom_point(aes(color = factor(ETH)), size=I(4)) +
  scale_color_brewer(type="seq", palette=7)


P + geom_point(aes(color = factor(ETH)), size=I(4)) +
  scale_color_brewer(palette="Reds")


P + geom_point(aes(color = factor(ETH)), size=I(4)) +
  scale_color_brewer(palette="Set1")
```

You can devise many other combinations of type and palette. Let's see the graph of the last command:

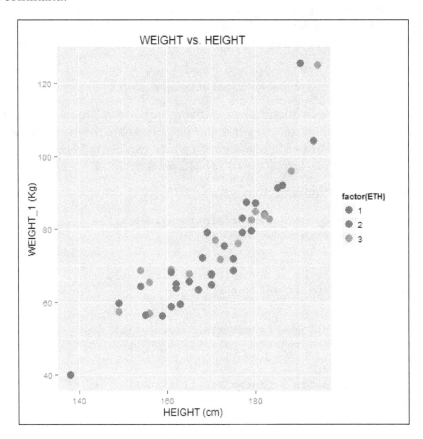

We have mapped attractive colors to each level of ethnicity.

Creating curves for each factor level

Let's see how to produce multiple curves in ggplot. We use the Children dataset (refer to the *Creating multiple curves simultaneously* section in *Chapter 3, Mastering the qplot Function*) to produce a line graph of height against age for each child. We created this particular graph in qplot and now we create it in ggplot, but we amend it a little. You can cut and paste the data directly from the code file for this chapter. Remember that the data for each child is arranged in a single column that holds six measurements of height for each child. We will include large points (size = 3) and slightly heavier lines (lwd = 1.2) using geom_point() and geom_line(), respectively. We will also map a color to the variable Child, so that both points and lines have a unique color for each child.

Finally, we impose our own color scheme using `scale_color_manual()`:

```
ggplot(cheight, aes(x=Age, y=Height, color = factor(Child))) +
  geom_point(size = 3) +  geom_line(lwd = 0.7) + labs(title =
    "Childrens' Growth Patterns") + labs(x = "Age (years)", y =
      "HEIGHT (cm)") + scale_color_manual(values = c("red",
        "yellow", "blue", "darkgreen"))
```

Now we get this graph:

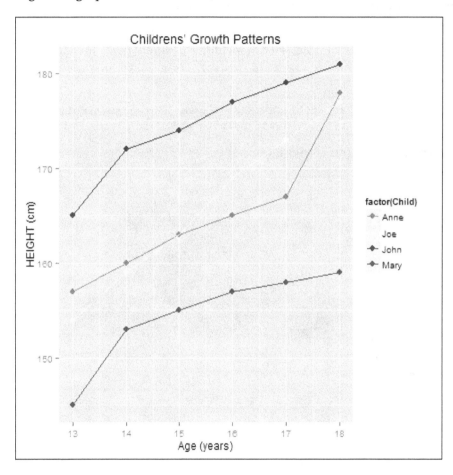

The arrangement of the data within a single column made it easy to create a graph with all four curves at once.

Creating histograms

In ggplot, we can create histograms using geom_histogram(). Histograms record frequencies for a continuous variable by dividing it into bins of a particular width. Using the medical dataset, use the following syntax to create a basic histogram of patient height, setting the bin width to 10 cm. Again, you can read the data by copying and pasting it from the code file for this chapter. The syntax is as follows:

```
ggplot(T, aes(x=HEIGHT)) + geom_histogram(binwidth=10)
```

Within a histogram, we may wish to identify subgroups of the population using different colors. In our example, we can include a different color for each gender using a color scheme from scale_fill_brewer(). Again, we use a bin width of 10 cm:

```
ggplot(T, aes(x=HEIGHT, fill=GENDER)) + geom_histogram(binwidth=10) +
  scale_fill_brewer(type = "div", palette = 4)
```

Here is what the histogram looks like:

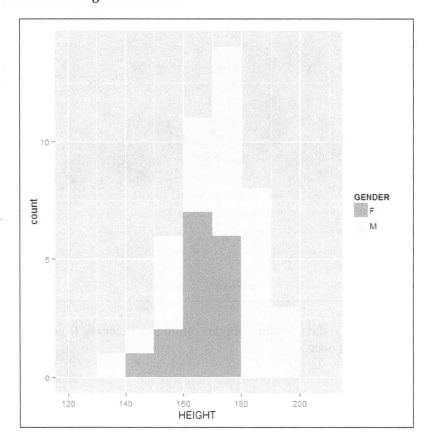

Essentially, we have two histograms together. This information is very useful, but perhaps a better alternative is to produce a grouped histogram using the argument `position = "dodge"`:

```
ggplot(T, aes(x=HEIGHT, fill=GENDER)) +
  geom_histogram(position="dodge", binwidth=10) +
    scale_fill_brewer(type = "qual", palette = 2)
```

This syntax gives the following histogram:

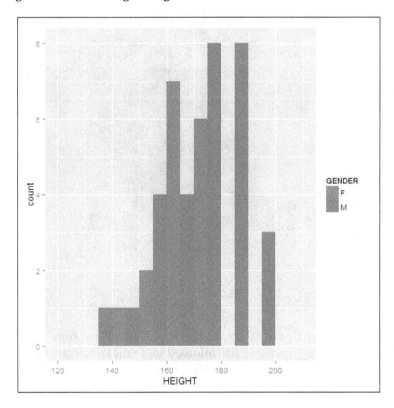

This grouped histogram has an attractive appearance and presents the information effectively. However, the bins look as though they represent 5 cm each. In fact, each bin represents 10 cm, but the histogram includes bars for both genders within each bin. Let's try a similar example, this time partitioning by ETH (a three-level categorical variable) and using a different color palette from `scale_fill_brewer()`. To achieve this graph, we include `factor(ETH)` to force a grouped histogram for three levels:

```
ggplot(T, aes(x=HEIGHT, fill=factor(ETH))) +
  geom_histogram(position="dodge", binwidth=10) +
    scale_fill_brewer(type = "qual", palette = 6)
```

Our histogram looks like this:

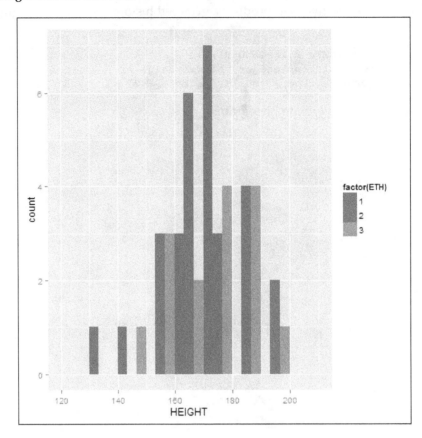

Again, the bin width remains at 10 cm, but now we have three bars within each bin. The use of `scale_color_brewer()` has allowed us to make effective and attractive histograms in which subgroups are identified by color.

Creating bar charts

Bar charts are useful for comparing the numbers of elements within subgroups of a population. However, they can be used for other purposes, such as comparing the means of a continuous variable across the levels of a categorical variable. You can create bar charts in `ggplot` using `geom_bar()`. As an exercise, create a bar chart of numbers of patients by ethnicity by turning the variable ETH into a factor by using `factor()`. The syntax is as follows:

```
W <- ggplot(T, aes(factor(ETH))) +  geom_bar()
W
```

The height of each bar gives the number of patients within each ethnicity. As an exercise, you can create a horizontal bar chart by adding the layer `coord_flip()`. The `coord_flip()` layer also works for other types of graph, including scatterplots and bar charts.

Now we insert our choice of color and border color using `fill` and `color`. Let's have an ivory color for the bars, along with dark green borders. The syntax is as follows:

```
W + geom_bar(fill="ivory", color="darkgreen")
```

This syntax gives the following bar chart:

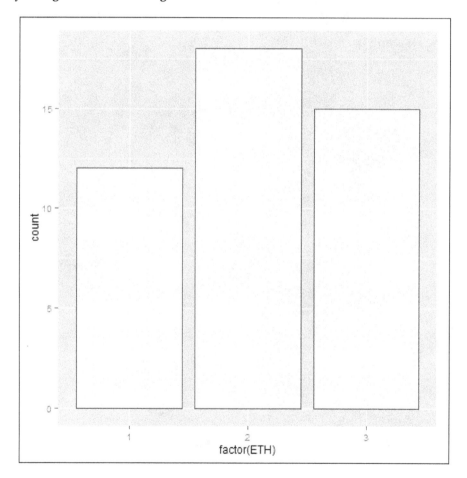

Creating a stacked bar chart

Now we will see how to create a stacked bar chart of a categorical variable, partitioned by the levels of another categorical variable. Let's plot the numbers of patients receiving each treatment, partitioned by the two levels of RECOVER. Simply insert both variables within aes(), mapping a color to one of them using fill and choosing our own colors using scale_fill_manual(). This time, we choose colors by entering colors(distinct = FALSE) on the command line and selecting from the list returned by R:

```
ggplot(T, aes(TREATMENT, fill=factor(RECOVER))) + geom_bar() +
  scale_fill_manual(values = c("springgreen3", " lightsalmon1"))
```

Here is the resulting bar chart:

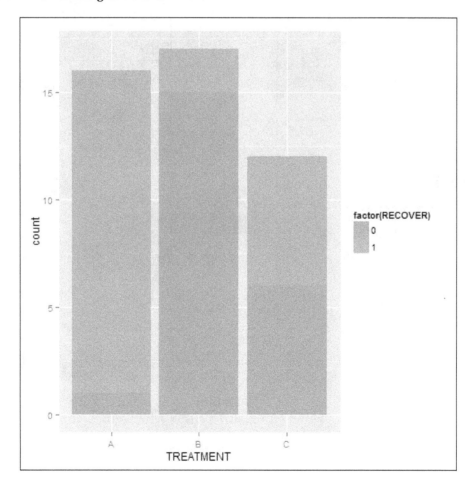

The label **0** represents patients who did not recover and the label **1** represents those who did recover. Thus, the stacked bar chart suggests that treatment A was the most effective, while treatment B was the least effective.

We can try faceting this bar chart to create separate charts for those who recover and those who do not. We use the syntax `facet_wrap(~ RECOVER)` in order to create separate graphs for each level of `RECOVER`. The `facet_wrap()` function is covered in more detail in the section entitled *Creating a faceted bar chart*. We choose our colors from the Hexadecimal Color Chart using `scale_fill_manual()`. Here, we subset for smokers only. The syntax is as follows

```
ggplot(subset(T, SMOKE == "Y"), aes(TREATMENT, fill=
   factor(RECOVER))) + geom_bar()+ facet_wrap(~ RECOVER) +
     scale_fill_manual(values = c("#669933", "#FFCC33"))
```

Now the bar chart looks like this:

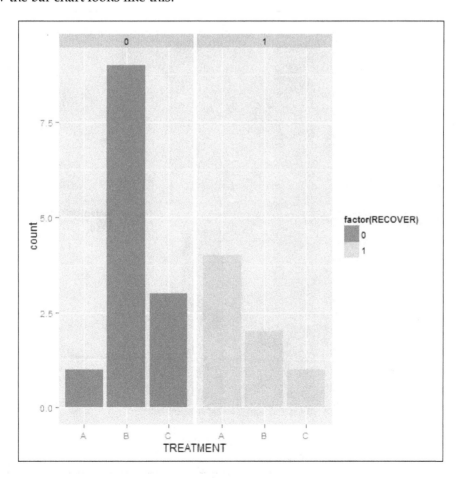

This bar chart gives us the required information, partitioned into two separate charts—one for each level of RECOVER.

Creating a grouped bar chart

We can present the same information using grouped bar chart. To do so, we use the argument position = "dodge" argument, again within geom_bar(). Again, we choose our colors from the Hexadecimal Color Chart using scale_fill_manual(). We subset for those who exercise. The syntax is as follows:

```
ggplot(subset(T, EXERCISE == "TRUE"), aes(TREATMENT, fill=
  factor(RECOVER))) + geom_bar(position="dodge") +
    scale_fill_manual(values = c("#6666FF", "#669900"))
```

You will get this bar chart:

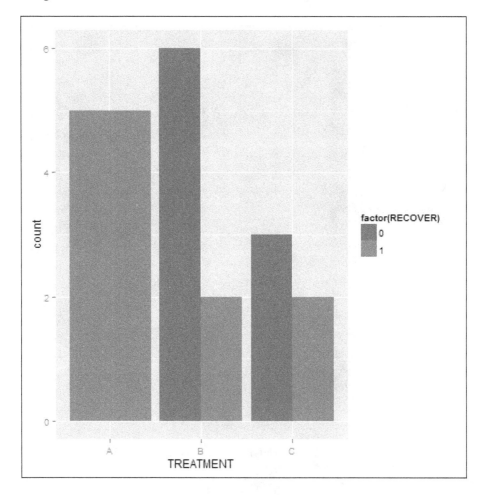

All patients who exercised and received treatment **A** eventually recovered. You can verify this result by examining this particular subset, as follows:

```
subset(T, EXERCISE == "TRUE" & TREATMENT == "A")
```

The output is as follows:

```
   PATIENT GENDER ETH TREATMENT AGE WEIGHT_1 WEIGHT_2 HEIGHT SMOKE EXERCISE RECOVER
1     Mary      F   1         A   Y     79.2     76.6    169     Y     TRUE       1
7  Charles      M   3         A   E     76.2     74.7    176     N     TRUE       1
11  Stuart      M   2         A   Y     67.7     65.3    170     N     TRUE       1
15     Sue      F   1         A   M     79.6     79.8    179     N     TRUE       1
33   Peter      M   1         A   M     79.1     76.8    177     N     TRUE       1
```

Creating a faceted bar chart

As a more complex example in which we include even more information, let's try a faceted bar chart of the numbers of patients receiving each treatment. However, the bar chart is now partitioned by both gender and stacked according to whether or not the patient recovered.

In fact, ggplot provides two functions to create facet plots. We use facet_grid() to split a variable by the levels of one or more categorical variables so that the graphs for each level are placed together, arranged either horizontally or vertically. We use facet_wrap() to position the facet plots together in your chosen number of rows and columns. For further information on these two functions, visit the following websites:

- To find helpful material on creating wrapped facet plots, refer to http://docs.ggplot2.org/0.9.3.1/facet_wrap.html

- To find out more about creating grid plots, refer to http://docs.ggplot2. org/0.9.3.1/facet_grid.html

Let's use facet_grid() on TREATMENT, faceted by the two levels of RECOVER:

```
ggplot(T, aes(TREATMENT, fill=factor(RECOVER))) + geom_bar() +
  facet_grid(. ~ GENDER) + scale_fill_manual(values =
    c("#339999","#CC9900"))
```

This syntax produces the following faceted bar chart:

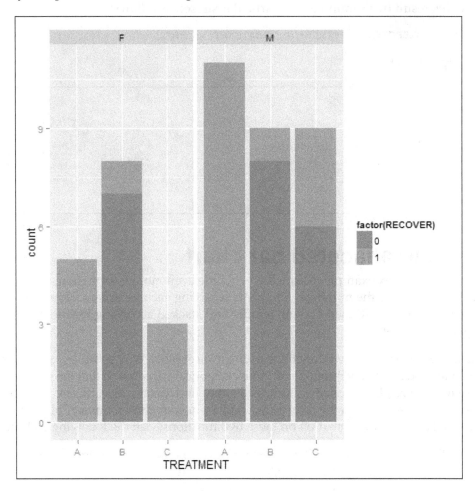

This graph presents a lot of useful information at once. Partitioning by gender allows us to compare patient recovery within and across the two genders and also within and across treatment levels.

Creating boxplots

In ggplot, we create boxplots using geom_boxplot(). Here, you will create a boxplot of the heights of female patients, partitioned by ethnicity. As in previous examples, we use the subset() command to include only females. We can create the subset either before we use ggplot, or within ggplot, as follows:

```
H <- ggplot(subset(T, GENDER == "F"), aes(factor(ETH), HEIGHT))
```

You can create a basic boxplot yourself by entering the following syntax:

```
H + geom_boxplot()
```

You should have got a basic boxplot of height, partitioned by ethnicity. For the remainder of this section, we will embellish our basic boxplot.

Try the following boxplots for yourself:

```
H + geom_boxplot() + geom_jitter()
H + geom_boxplot() + coord_flip()
H + geom_boxplot(outlier.color = "red", outlier.size =
   5)
H + geom_boxplot(aes(fill = SMOKE))
H + geom_boxplot(fill= "#99CCFF" , color="#990000")
```

Next we set our choice of fill color and outline color from the Hexadecimal Color Chart, using the following syntax:

```
H + geom_boxplot(aes(fill = factor(ETH))) + scale_fill_manual(values
   = c("#CCCC99","#FFCCCC","#99CCFF"))
```

You will get this boxplot:

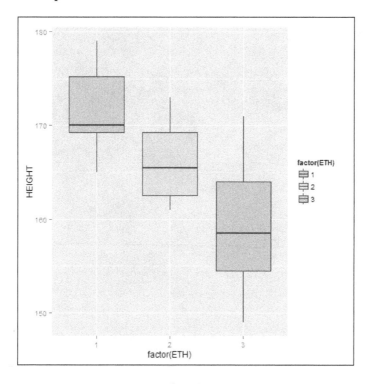

Labeling points with text

Now we will see how to label points with text. Suppose that we want a graph of the heights of treatment A female patients against their weight before treatment, in which each point is labeled by the patient's name and where the text is in red. First we subset using the `subset()` command, but we include two criteria (gender and treatment). We include the text using the function `geom_text()`. Remember that the variable `PATIENT` gave the names of each patient. Enter the following syntax:

```
F <- subset(T, GENDER == "F" & TREATMENT == "A")
S <- ggplot(F, aes(x=HEIGHT, y=WEIGHT_1, label=PATIENT))
```

Finally, we add the required text, but we do not include the points as yet:

```
S + geom_text(size = 6, col = "red")
```

The following graph shows the names of the patients:

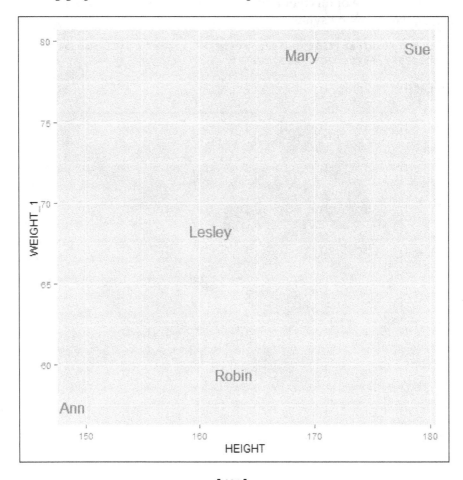

In the preceding graph, the patients' names appeared without any points. Of course, we can set text aesthetics to our chosen values. As an exercise, use the following syntax to create a graph with point labels. You use blue text and position the text underneath and to the left of the points using `hjust= 1` and `vjust= 1`:

```
S + geom_point() + geom_text(hjust=1, vjust=1, size = 6, col =
  "blue")
```

Note that one name was cut off (**Ann**). We will learn how to fix that problem in the next example. The arguments `hjust` and `vjust` vary the position of the text relative to the points; `hjust` allows you to control horizontal justification, while `vjust` allows you to control vertical justification. Both `hjust` and `vjust` range between 0 and 1, where 0 gives left-justified text and 1 produces right-justified text. Try different values of `hjust` and `vjust` yourself. For example, using the value zero places the text above and to the right.

You can also experiment with the text size and angle. In the following example, you set `hjust` and `vjust` to zero:

```
S + geom_point() + geom_text(angle = 45, hjust=0, vjust=0, size = 6,
  col = "darkgreen")
```

If you created this graph, you will have noticed that two names were cut off (**Mary** and **Sue**). To fix this problem, we can reset the axis limits to include both names using `scale_x_continuous()` and `scale_y_continuous()`. We choose axis limits that ensure the inclusion of both names. For the vertical axis, we can choose 50 Kg to 100 Kg, and for the horizontal axis we can choose 140 cm to 200 cm.

```
S + geom_point() + geom_text(angle = 45, hjust=0, vjust=0, size = 6,
  col = "darkgreen") +  scale_y_continuous(limits=c(50, 100)) +
    scale_x_continuous(limits=c(140, 200))
```

Here is our graph:

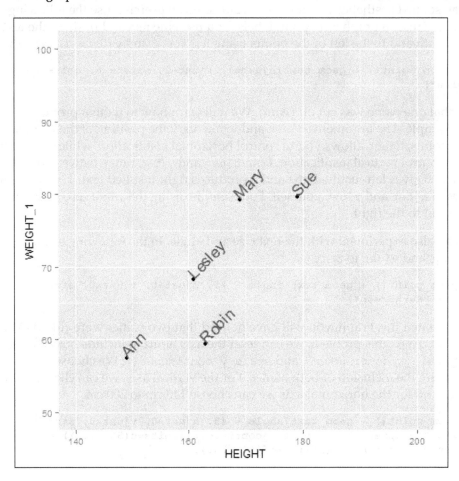

Now each name appears in full. Of course, we could have chosen other axis limits that included all of the patients' names.

Mapping color to text

Next, we will learn how to map color to text for categorical variables. In this example, you map text color to the variable ETH. Again, you do so within aes() by turning ETH into a factor:

```
S + geom_text(aes(color=factor(ETH)))
```

You will see that the patient's names now appear in a different color for each ethnicity. For the next example, we put the text at an angle of 35 degrees and justify the text. We retain suitable axis limits to include all names in full. We also choose a color scheme using `scale_color_brewer()`. Finally, we rename and relabel the legend entries appropriately using `name` and `labels`. The syntax is as follows:

```
S + geom_point() + geom_text(aes(color=factor(ETH), angle = 35,
  hjust=1, vjust=1)) +  scale_y_continuous(limits=c(50, 90)) +
    scale_x_continuous(limits=c(140, 190)) +
      scale_color_brewer(palette= "Set1" , name =
        "Ethnicity",labels=c("European","Asian","Other"))
```

This syntax will give the following graph:

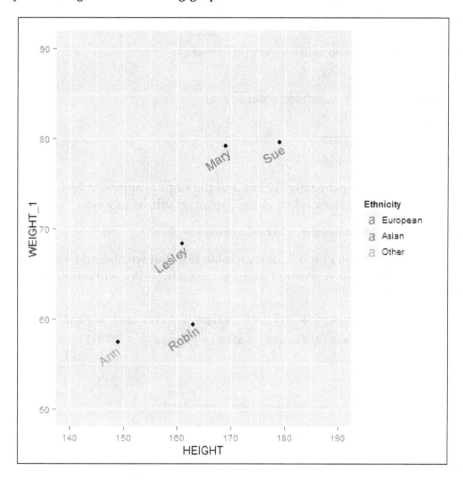

Mapping text color to the categorical variable ETH has conveyed additional information about these patients.

Including regression lines

In ggplot, you can include regression lines using geom_abline(). For the next example, we set up the same graph of patient height against weight that we have used several times before:

```
P <- ggplot(T, aes(x = HEIGHT, y = WEIGHT_1)) + geom_point()
```

As a start, let's calculate the slope and intercept of the line of best fit (regression line) for height against weight before treatment. In *Chapter 1, Base Graphics in R – One Step at a Time*, in the section entitled *Including a regression line*, we saw how to include a linear regression line on a graph. Now, we use the lm() command again to fit a linear regression model by using the following syntax:

```
lm(WEIGHT_1 ~ HEIGHT, data = T)
```

Here is the output that you will see on your screen:

```
Call:
lm(formula = WEIGHT_1 ~ HEIGHT, data = T)
Coefficients:
(Intercept)        HEIGHT
   -123.611         1.166
```

So, the intercept is approximately -123.61 and the slope is approximately 1.17. You can now include the regression line in the ggplot graph, as follows:

```
P + geom_abline(intercept = -123.61, slope = 1.17)
```

Now we will recreate the graph with regression line, but we also add some descriptive text about the regression using geom_text(). We will center the text on the point (170, 110).

```
P + geom_abline(intercept = -123.61, slope = 1.17, col = "red") +
geom_text(data = T, aes(170, 110, label = "Slope = 1.17"))
```

The graph with regression line looks like the following one:

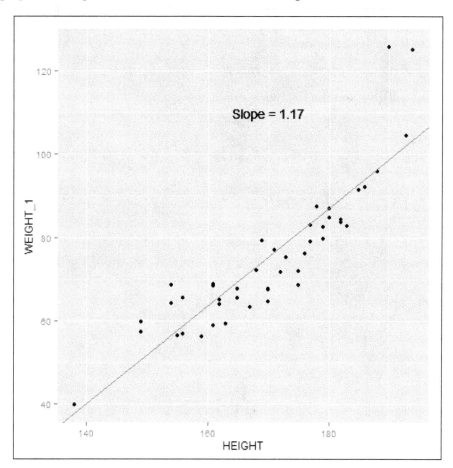

Your text is indeed centered on the point (170, 110). The approach we used to create the regression line was quite straightforward, but it is easier to use `stat_smooth()`. This function allows you to use smoothers on your graph, including OLS regressions, generalized linear models, and LOWESS smoothers. You can read further about this function on `http://docs.ggplot2.org/0.9.3.1/stat_smooth.html`.

In the final examples of this book, we try an OLS regression using the argument `method="lm"`. This approach is more efficient than the previous approach, because we can implement it in a single step. First, let's try switching off the standard error using the following command:

```
P + stat_smooth(method="lm", se=FALSE)
```

This syntax will give you the following graph:

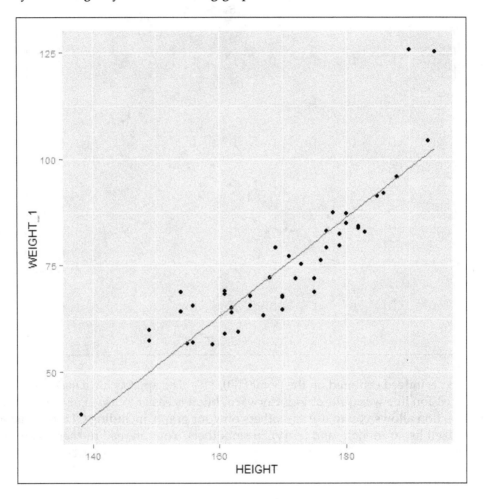

Next, we switch on the standard error:

```
P + stat_smooth(method="lm", se=TRUE)
```

We get the following graph:

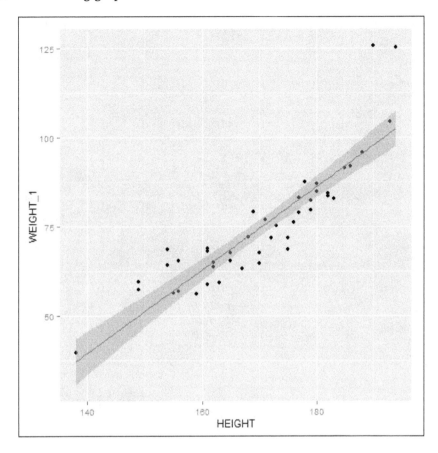

Our graph now includes a confidence band whose width is determined by the standard error. The `stat_smooth()` function provides a range of smoothers that can be implemented easily using the `method` argument.

Summary

In this chapter, you encountered `ggplot` for the first time. You learned how to set up your variables for plotting and how to control symbol type, color, size, and shape. You learned how to create bar charts, histograms, and boxplots using `ggplot`. You also learned about a range of methods for customizing lines, point labels and smoothers. These methods should enable you to create a wide range of graphs that are suitable for publication. Perhaps you found that `ggplot` is more difficult to master than `qplot`. However, you should also have found that `ggplot` offers great scope for creating high-quality graphs.

Index

K

kernel density plots
creating 121-123

L

labs() function
using 141
las argument 25
legend
creating 62
levels() command 85
line graphs
creating, qplot used 108-110
line plots
creating 12, 13
lines() command 8, 72
lm() command 38
LOWESS (locally weighted scatterplot smoothing) 88

M

mathematical expressions
including, on plots 30, 31
mathematical functions
graphing 19
medical dataset
for creating graphs 41-43
melt() function 134
mtext() command 45
multiple curves
creating simultaneously 111, 112
multiple graphs
creating, on same page 27, 28

O

objects
graphs, setting up as 105, 106
Ordinary Least Squares (OLS) regressions 18

P

parameter values
passing, to labels 15-17

passing, to titles 15-17
paste() command 15, 30
pdf() command 28
pie charts
creating 76-80
pie() command 78
plot() command 6, 35
point labels
creating 47, 48
points
creating 10, 11
joining 10, 11
points, graphs with ggplot
labeling with text 164, 165
polygon() command
about 51, 122
used, for shading normal curve 55-58
predict() command 38

Q

qplot
about 95
used, for creating histograms 118, 119
used, for creating line graphs 108-110
used, for producing scatterplots 96-98
qplot syntax
about 96
arguments 96
Quick-R
URL 7

R

R
bar charts, creating 58-61
basic graphics techniques 6-9
color palettes 88
colors 14
datasets, reading 34
options 20, 21
range() command 73
read.csv() command 63
regression line
including 18, 34-40
regression lines, graphs with ggplot
including 168-171

Thank you for buying
R Graph Essentials

About Packt Publishing

Packt, pronounced 'packed', published its first book "*Mastering phpMyAdmin for Effective MySQL Management*" in April 2004 and subsequently continued to specialize in publishing highly focused books on specific technologies and solutions.

Our books and publications share the experiences of your fellow IT professionals in adapting and customizing today's systems, applications, and frameworks. Our solution based books give you the knowledge and power to customize the software and technologies you're using to get the job done. Packt books are more specific and less general than the IT books you have seen in the past. Our unique business model allows us to bring you more focused information, giving you more of what you need to know, and less of what you don't.

Packt is a modern, yet unique publishing company, which focuses on producing quality, cutting-edge books for communities of developers, administrators, and newbies alike. For more information, please visit our website: www.packtpub.com.

About Packt Open Source

In 2010, Packt launched two new brands, Packt Open Source and Packt Enterprise, in order to continue its focus on specialization. This book is part of the Packt Open Source brand, home to books published on software built around Open Source licenses, and offering information to anybody from advanced developers to budding web designers. The Open Source brand also runs Packt's Open Source Royalty Scheme, by which Packt gives a royalty to each Open Source project about whose software a book is sold.

Writing for Packt

We welcome all inquiries from people who are interested in authoring. Book proposals should be sent to author@packtpub.com. If your book idea is still at an early stage and you would like to discuss it first before writing a formal book proposal, contact us; one of our commissioning editors will get in touch with you.

We're not just looking for published authors; if you have strong technical skills but no writing experience, our experienced editors can help you develop a writing career, or simply get some additional reward for your expertise.

R Graphs Cookbook

ISBN: 978-1-84951-306-7   Paperback: 272 pages

Detailed hands-on recipes for creating the most useful types of graphs in R — starting from the simplest versions to more advanced applications

1. Learn to draw any type of graph or visual data representation in R.

2. Filled with practical tips and techniques for creating any type of graph you need; not just theoretical explanations.

3. All examples are accompanied with the corresponding graph images, so you know what the results look like.

Statistical Analysis with R

ISBN: 978-1-84951-208-4   Paperback: 300 pages

Take control of your data and produce superior statistical analyses with R

1. An easy introduction for people who are new to R, with plenty of strong examples for you to work through.

2. This book will take you on a journey to learn R as the strategist for an ancient Chinese kingdom!

3. A step-by-step guide to understand R, its benefits, and how to use it to maximize the impact of your data analysis.

Please check **www.PacktPub.com** for information on our titles

Learning RStudio for R Statistical Computing

ISBN: 978-1-78216-060-1   Paperback: 126 pages

Learn to effectively perform R development, statistical analysis, and reporting with the most popular R IDE

1. A complete practical tutorial for RStudio, designed keeping in mind the needs of analysts and R developers alike.

2. Step-by-step examples that apply the principles of reproducible research and good programming practices to R projects.

3. Learn to effectively generate reports, create graphics, and perform analysis, and even build R-packages with RStudio.

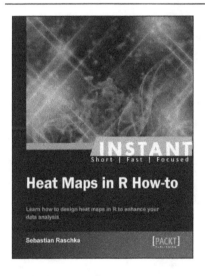

Instant Heat Maps in R How-to

ISBN: 978-1-78216-564-4   Paperback: 72 pages

Learn how to design heat maps in R to enhance your data analysis

1. Learn something new in an Instant! A short, fast, focused guide delivering immediate results.

2. Create heat maps in R using different file formats.

3. Learn how to make choropleth maps and contour plots.

4. Generate your own customized heat maps and add interactivity for displaying on the web.

Please check **www.PacktPub.com** for information on our titles